The Prussian Army of Frederick the Great, 1740–1786

Gabriele Esposito is a military historian who works as a freelance author and researcher for some of the most important publishing houses in the military history sector. In particular, he is an expert specializing in uniformology: his interests and expertise range from the ancient civilizations to modern post-colonial conflicts. During recent years, he has conducted and published several researches on the military history of the Latin American countries, with special attention on the War of the Triple Alliance and the War of the Pacific. He is among the leading experts on the military history of the Italian Wars of Unification and the Spanish Carlist Wars. His books and essays are published on a regular basis by Osprey Publishing, Winged Hussar Publishing and Libreria Editrice Goriziana. He is also the author of numerous military history articles appearing in specialized magazines such as *Ancient Warfare Magazine*, *Medieval Warfare Magazine*, *The Armourer*, *History of War*, *Guerres et Histoire*, *Focus Storia* and *Focus Storia Wars*.

The Prussian Army of Frederick the Great, 1740–1786

History, Organization and Uniforms

Gabriele Esposito

Pen & Sword
MILITARY

First published in Great Britain in 2024 by
Pen & Sword Military
An imprint of
Pen & Sword Books Limited
Yorkshire – Philadelphia

ISBN 978 1 39905 185 9

A CIP catalogue record for this book is
available from the British Library

Typeset by Mac Style
Printed and bound in India by Parksons Graphics Pvt. Ltd.

Pen & Sword Books Limited incorporates the imprints of After the Battle,
Atlas, Archaeology, Aviation, Discovery, Family History, Fiction, History,
Maritime, Military, Military Classics, Politics, Select, Transport, True Crime,
Air World, Frontline Publishing, Leo Cooper, Remember When, Seaforth
Publishing, The Praetorian Press, Wharncliffe Local History, Wharncliffe
Transport, Wharncliffe True Crime and White Owl.

For a complete list of Pen & Sword titles please contact:

PEN & SWORD BOOKS LIMITED
47 Church Street, Barnsley, South Yorkshire, S70 2AS, England
E-mail: enquiries@pen-and-sword.co.uk
Website: www.pen-and-sword.co.uk
or
PEN AND SWORD BOOKS
1950 Lawrence Rd, Havertown, PA 19083, USA
E-mail: uspen-and-sword@casematepublishers.com
Website: www.penandswordbooks.com

Contents

Acknowledgements

This book is dedicated to my parents, Maria Rosaria and Benedetto, for the immense love and great support that they give me during all the days of my life. A very special thanks goes to Philip Sidnell, the commissioning editor of my books for Pen & Sword: his love for military history and his passion for publishing are fundamental for the success of our publications. A special mention goes to the production manager of this title, Matt Jones, for his hard work and great competence. Many thanks also to copy-editor Tony Walton, for his precious help and for his friendship. Most of the pictures published in this book are in the public domain, obtained from the magnificent Digital Collections of the New York Public Library. Anyone with an interest in military history can easily browse the vast contents of the collection at https://digitalcollections.nypl.org/.

Introduction

The main aim of this book is to provide a detailed overview of the history, organization and uniforms of Frederick the Great's formidable Prussian Army, which was without doubt one of the most famous fighting forces in history, capable of achieving numerous iconic victories under the leadership of its leader. Although Frederick the Great transformed Prussia into the most important of the German states and one of Europe's leading Great Powers of the eighteenth century, he was not a lover of war or of military life, preferring the arts (music in particular) culture and philosophy. He inherited the basic structures of Prussian militarism from his father, Frederick William I, who had worked hard to improve the standards of service of the Prussian Army. Thanks to his intelligence and political vision, Frederick used this excellent military apparatus to expand the boundaries of Prussia. He fought three major wars against the Austrian Empire of the Habsburgs in order to secure possession over the rich region of Silesia, during which he obtained many glorious victories, as well as some humiliating defeats. Being a great tactician and innovator, Frederick revolutionized warfare and changed the political balance of Europe thanks to the valour of his battle-hardened soldiers. We will describe the major military campaigns fought by the Prussian Army during Frederick's long reign of 1740–86, from the First Silesian War to the little-known and inconclusive War of the Bavarian Succession of 1778–79. We will also detail the organization, uniforms and equipment of the various branches of service that made up the Prussian Army. We will start with the infantry, which formed the backbone of Frederick the Great's armies thanks to its incredible discipline and excellent training. The Prussian foot soldiers – be they fusiliers, musketeers or grenadiers – showed great valour during dozens of pitched battles and defeated many different enemies. They soon became iconic, exactly like their king, with their austere lifestyle and dark blue uniforms. We will also feature the guard units of the Prussian infantry – including the famous 'Potsdam Giants', also known as the 'Giant Guard of Potsdam' – and some little-known foot corps, such as the garrison units that performed auxiliary military duties or the light infantry Jagers. We will then turn our attention towards the Prussian cavalry, which included some guard formations as well as regiments belonging to four different specialities: cuirassiers, dragoons, hussars and lancers. The cuirassiers were the heavy cavalry component of the Prussian Army, tasked with conducting frontal charges, while the dragoons were a medium cavalry that could perform a variety of different duties. The hussars, meanwhile, were tasked with scouting and skirmishing, being accomplished light cavalrymen, and the lancers consisted of a single elite corps recruited from Balkan soldiers and had a very distinctive uniform. An entire chapter of the book will be devoted to the technical corps of the Prussian Army, most notably the artillery, but also some minor branches of service like the engineers and the pioneers. During his wars, Frederick the Great frequently employed large numbers of mercenaries, which were organized into special units known as 'Frei-Corps', or 'Free Corps'. These came from different areas of Europe and were mostly equipped as light infantry or light cavalry. We will cover their history in detail and provide descriptions of their extravagant uniforms. In the last chapter of the book, we will focus on the military contingents that were provided to Frederick the Great by his German allies of Brunswick, Hanover and Hesse-Kassel.

Chapter 1

The Ascendancy of Prussia

The early history of Prussia is a complex one, dating back to the last decades of the Middle Ages. In 1411, after having been defeated by the Polish-Lithuanian state, the Teutonic Order had to renounce several of the territories that it had conquered in the Baltic area. The Teutonic Order, one of the most famous military orders created during the Crusades for the liberation of the Holy Land from Muslim rule, had established itself on the north-eastern borders of the German Holy Roman Empire after the end of the Crusades. Here, since the middle of the thirteenth century, it had started to campaign against the local pagan peoples, with the main objective of transforming the Slavs of the Baltic into Christians. Supported by both the Holy Roman Empire and the Papacy, the Teutonic Knights gradually established their own state on the north-eastern borders of Germany after fighting several wars against the local peoples and the most important regional power of the area: the Kingdom of Poland. Despite being a Christian state, Poland became the fiercest enemy of the Teutonic Order; after it was united with Lithuania, Poland became powerful enough to challenge the political supremacy exerted by the Teutonic Order over the Baltic. The final and decisive conflict between the Polish-Lithuanian state and the Teutonic Knights took place between 1409 and 1411, and ended in a clear victory for the Poles and Lithuanians. Consequently, during the following century, although the Teutonic state continued to exist as an autonomous political entity, it lost most of its previous importance and had to recognize – at least formally – the overlordship of Poland-Lithuania. From 1519–21, while most of the Holy Roman Empire was ravaged by the political events caused by the Protestant Reformation, the Teutonic state and Poland-Lithuania fought each other in a new war. This conflict also ended in defeat for the Teutonic Knights, who were forced to abandon any remaining ambition of revenge directed against Poland. In 1525, the last Grand Master of the Teutonic Order, Albert of Brandenburg-Ansbach, agreed to secularize the Teutonic state and to transform it into the new Duchy of Prussia. Albert assumed the title of Duke of Prussia and his new state, no longer ruled by a Catholic military order, was a vassal of Poland-Lithuania. The first Duke of Prussia confirmed his decisions by adopting Lutheranism in 1525, which ended forever the existence of the Teutonic Order.

Colour plate showing the uniforms of the King's Regiment under the rule of Frederick William I. The grenadier on the left has the uniform worn by the 1st Battalion, the grenadier on the right that worn by the 2nd Battalion and 3rd Battalion.

Albert was a member of the Brandenburg-Ansbach branch of the House of Hohenzollern, which was one of the most important noble families of the Holy Roman Empire, controlling territories in the western portion of the Holy Roman Empire (in Franconia) as well as the Margraviate of Brandenburg in north-eastern Germany. In 1618, the year that saw the outbreak of the bloody Thirty Years' War in the Holy Roman Empire, the Duchy of Prussia was inherited by the ruling Margrave of Brandenburg; as a result, from that moment on, the Duchy of Prussia and the Margraviate of Brandenburg were ruled by the same person in a 'personal union'. The members of the Brandenburg-Ansbach family found themselves in a difficult political position, since they were members of the Holy Roman Empire as Margraves of Brandenburg but also vassals of Poland-Lithuania as dukes of Prussia. From a social point of view, the two states of Brandenburg and Prussia were quite different: Brandenburg had several important urban centres and did not have a strong nobility, whereas Prussia was dominated by a powerful landed nobility – whose members were known as *junkers* – who owned great estates worked by peasants with very few rights. The *junkers* were the heirs of the Teutonic Knights and controlled the vast agricultural areas of Prussia, which were inhabited by poor peasants who were the descendants of the Slavs defeated by the Teutonic Order. During the second half of the seventeenth century, the rulers of Brandenburg-Prussia tried to conquer that portion of Poland that divided their Brandenburg territories from the Prussian ones, but they were thwarted by strong Polish opposition. In 1654, however, the Duchy of Prussia ceased to be a vassal of Poland-Lithuania. During the last years of the century, Brandenburg-Prussia became increasingly important from a political point of view, mostly due to the intelligent diplomatic choices of its ruler, Frederick III.

Being one of the most powerful nobles in Germany, Frederick III wanted to have the prestigious title of 'king' for himself and his heirs. This, however, was not possible according to the laws that governed Germany at the time, since the only kingdom that could exist within the Holy Roman Empire was that of Bohemia (which belonged to the Holy Roman Emperor). Yet this was valid for Brandenburg only, since Prussia was not part of the Holy Roman Empire. As a result, in 1700, Frederick III asked Holy Roman Emperor Leopold I to allow Prussia to be elevated to the status of kingdom. Leopold, who was already fighting Louis XIV's France in the bloody War of the Spanish Succession, badly needed strong allies like Frederick III and thus – in 1701 – permitted Frederick to be crowned as King of Prussia. Prussia thereafter started to emerge as a strong player in the politics of both Germany and the Baltic. During the years 1701–21, Brandenburg-Prussia – simply known as Prussia since 1701 – fought two wars at the same time. In Western Europe, it participated in the War of the Spanish Succession by providing 8,000 soldiers to Leopold I for his

Colour plate showing the uniforms worn by the Prussian infantry under Frederick William I. From left to right: musketeer of the 1st Infantry Regiment, musketeer of the 21st Infantry Regiment and grenadier of the 5th Infantry Regiment.

struggle against Louis XIV. Meanwhile, in Eastern Europe, it took part in the Great Northern War, a conflict that was extremely important for the history of the Baltic region, which had been dominated by Sweden since the end of the Thirty Years' War in 1648. In 1700, the various regional enemies of the Swedes – the emerging Russia of Peter the Great, Denmark-Norway and Saxony-Poland – formed a strong military alliance in a bid to expel Sweden from the southern portion of the Baltic. Prussia joined the anti-Swedish alliance only in 1715, when it was already apparent that Russia was gaining the upper hand in the conflict. With the peace treaties that followed Sweden's defeat and the end of the Great Northern War, the Kingdom of Prussia obtained the southern portion of Pomerania (a rich region of north-eastern Germany that had previously been part of the Swedish Baltic domains). The political emergence of Prussia was made possible by the contemporary decline of three military powers that had previously been very important: the Holy Roman Empire, the Polish-Lithuanian Commonwealth and the Kingdom of Sweden. The Holy Roman Empire was greatly weakened by its internal political fragmentation, caused by the autonomist ambitions of the German princedoms, while the Polish-Lithuanian Commonwealth suffered due to its chronic political instability, which was caused by the frequent revolts of the major Polish nobles. Sweden, meanwhile, ceased to be a great power following the heavy defeats it suffered during the Great Northern War. This not only resulted in the ascendancy of Prussia, but also – probably more importantly – that of Russia. Until the rise to prominence of Tsar Peter the Great at the end of the seventeenth century, the Russian Empire had been a quite isolated and under-developed state that had very little in common with Europe. Under Peter's rule, the Russians modernized and 'westernized' their state and their military forces, to the point of becoming a fundamental player in the politics of both the Baltic and Poland-Lithuania. Surrounded by rival states that had major military resources at their disposal, Prussia had no choice but to develop a very strong army from the closing decades of the seventeenth century. This process, initiated by Frederick III, was continued by his son and successor, Frederick William I (who was King of Prussia from 1713).

Chapter 2

The Reign of the Soldier King

Frederick William I was a very particular monarch, quite different from all the others who ruled the European states of the time. As soon as he became king, he sold most of his father's jewels and horses in order to have enough money to expand his army. Frederick William had a personal lifestyle that was comparable to that of an ancient Spartan: it was frugal, austere, martial and heavily influenced by the Calvinist faith of the monarch. Frederick William did not love the pleasures of life, and instead spent his entire existence pursuing the interests of his kingdom. He practiced rigid management of the treasury, established schools and hospitals, encouraged farming and production of grain, reformed the administration of his country and reorganized the state's military forces. Frederick William ruled as an absolute monarch, thanks to the fact that he formed a strong political and social alliance with the *junkers*. He preserved the privileges of the *junkers* in exchange for their decisive support in case of war. Frederick William, however, was also intelligent enough to realize that a new middle class was also emerging in Prussia, which, if well integrated into Prussian society, could have contributed to the economic flourishing of the Prussian state. As a result, the monarch decided to favour the development of the middle class by replacing the compulsory military service required of its members with payment of an annual tax that was used for funding the expansion of the army. Due to his peculiar lifestyle and great military knowledge, Frederick William was known as the 'Soldier King'. His reform of Prussia's military was remarkable from many points of view as he transformed the Prussian Army into one of the deadliest war machines that the world had ever seen.

In 1733, Frederick William reorganized the Prussian military by introducing the 'Canton System'. According to this, the territory of Brandenburg-Prussia was divided into recruiting districts known as cantons, each of which latter was responsible for the formation of one regiment. A single canton comprised a variable number of 'fireplaces', or households, and was divided into districts comprising from a minimum of seven to a maximum of ten villages. Around 5,000 fireplaces were needed to raise an infantry regiment, while around 1,800 would raise a cavalry regiment. Each district was to provide a single company. The new system replaced both coercive recruiting and the hiring of expensive mercenary forces, two methods of recruitment that had

Officer (left) and grenadier (right) of the Grenadier-Garde Battalion.

been widely employed before 1733 but had been shown to have great limitations. The responsibility for recruitment operations was transferred from civilian authorities to regimental officers, all of whom were *junkers*, controlling large estates and needing peasant labour to have their land properties prosper. In order to meet the recruitment obligations assigned to them, before 1733, the junkers had two options: they could oblige their peasants to enlist or could recruit soldiers from abroad. The first option had very negative consequences for them, since all peasants had to continue working on the estates of the *junkers* if the latter wanted to keep their agricultural activities flourishing. The second option was extremely costly for the Prussian nobles, since they were obliged to spend large sums of money paying the required number of foreign mercenaries. The new Canton System was a response to these problems, since it introduced a form of regulated conscription that was quite modern for the time and permitted the formation of standing military forces. The Prussian conscripts were usually enrolled or registered by the pastor of their community on the occasion of their confirmation; the military registers of each canton were thus updated annually. Enrolled individuals, aged between 16 and 24, could be drafted every year as part of the annual inspection that took place every spring in time of peace. During this inspection, those young males who did not reach the height of at least 1.73 metres or who had already exceeded the age limit could be either assigned to one of the garrison regiments (a sort of reserve, having static military duties) or be completely released from military enrolment. The duration of the military service obligation was lifelong on paper, but in practice it lasted up to twenty years.

All the male individuals who had been enrolled were soon given a leave of absence from their commanding officers. Then, for the next twenty years, they were to train just two months every year in time of peace and could spend the remaining ten months working as peasants at home without receiving any pay from the government. Several social categories were exempt from military service, especially those that were not dominated by the *junkers*: nobles, members of the clergy, Mennonite Christians, craft traders and residents of the cities. The new Canton System had many positive aspects. For instance, it eliminated the violent methods previously employed to recruit peasants and gave equal treatment to the lower classes of society. It also preserved the economic viability of the various territories, which prevented mass desertion. The new recruiting system was one of the foundations of Prussian militarism, with the great majority of Prussian subjects being made part of a vast military system since 1733. In time of war, however, it was difficult for the communities living in a canton to replace the losses suffered by their regiment, since each soldier killed had to be replaced by his son or younger brother, which had a devastating impact on individual families. This – in time of crisis – resulted in a rural exodus, with the mass migration of peasant families from rural villages to major urban centres, as the inhabitants of the cities were exempt from military service. Prussian military discipline was extremely strict: when a soldier deserted, his son or younger brother was forced to replace him, exactly as if he had died. In addition, the entire property of the deserter could be confiscated by the state. Any violation of compulsory service was punishable as treason, and executions were quite common. Thanks to the introduction of the Canton System, Frederick William I could rapidly assemble a large standing army despite being the ruler of a country that had a relatively small population.

The Soldier King did not limit his military reforms to the introduction of a new recruiting system, as he also greatly modernized the training of his infantry. He introduced intensive training and harsh discipline that were aimed at increasing the Prussian infantrymen's rate of fire, and also sponsored the adoption of some innovative pieces of equipment, such as the iron ramrod that simplified the use of the standard flintlock musket. Frederick William I wanted his son, the future Frederick II (the Great), to become a fine soldier. He tried to educate him in a Spartan way, but with little success: Frederick was more interested in music and French culture than in supervising the training of his military forces. The relationship between father and son became increasingly difficult with the progression of time, to the point that the young prince was first imprisoned and then temporarily exiled from 1731–32.

In 1701, the Prussian Army of Frederick III included the following units: one company of Swiss Guards, one battalion of Prussian Guards, two companies of Gendarmes, two squadrons of Garde du Corps, two regiments and one battalion of Foot Guards, sixteen regiments of line infantry, nine regiments of cuirassiers, four regiments of dragoons and ten companies of artillery (one of bombardiers and nine of gunners). The Swiss Guard ('Schweizer Garde') was formed in 1696 and consisted of just 100 soldiers, dressed in the livery of the Hohenzollern family and armed with halberds. Members of this formation guarded the court and were entirely recruited from the Protestant cantons of Switzerland (the sovereigns of Prussia were the main 'champions' of the German Protestants). The Prussian Guard was the foot bodyguard of Frederick III and consisted of just five companies. The Gendarmes were created in 1691, initially being the 3rd Squadron of the Garde du Corps (which had been formed in 1687). Both these small cavalry corps acted as a noble honour guard for the Prussian monarchs; members of the Garde du Corps were commonly known as Trabanten or Grands Mousquetaires, since they were dressed very similarly to the contemporary French Royal Musketeers. The Gendarmes, instead, were equipped as cuirassiers. The two regiments of Foot Guards were the elite of the Prussian Army. The first was commonly known as the Leib-Garde Regiment and had been created in 1655. Initially it had an impressive establishment of thirty companies (organized

NCO (left), grenadier (centre) and officer (right) of the Grenadier-Garde Battalion.

on six battalions), but these were reduced to twenty-five in 1703 and then to fifteen in 1707. The second guard regiment was created in 1676 from four detached companies of the Leib-Garde Regiment; the unit had ten companies and was considered as the personal regiment of Dorothea of Brandenburg (consort of the Prussian prince and future king Frederick III). The single guard battalion was raised in 1698 from the Leib-Garde Regiment and was known as the Weisse Grenadier-Garde. In 1703, this unit became a regiment after absorbing the battalion of Prussian Guards, which ceased to exist as an autonomous corps. In 1707, Frederick III (formally Frederick I of Prussia since 1701) ordered the creation of a new Foot Guard regiment, which was formed with ten companies detached from the Leib-Garde Regiment. The Prussian line infantry regiments consisted of two battalions, with five companies each. There were no separate grenadier companies, but each fusilier company included a certain number of grenadiers. The cuirassier regiments had three squadrons each, these being structured on two companies. The dragoon regiments each had four squadrons of two companies.

The ambitious Frederick William I started to reform the Prussian Army when he was still a prince: in 1688, he became commander of one of the line infantry regiments, the Crown Prince Regiment. Traditionally, this corps was one of the best of the Prussian Army, albeit not being a guard regiment; it had long been commanded by the heirs to the Prussian throne. Frederick William soon began to improve the quality of his regiment and gradually transformed it into an innovative formation. In 1710, he ordered the creation of an independent grenadier battalion, known as the Red Battalion (from the colour of its uniform's facings) or the Unranked Battalion (since it was not given a number). This experimental corps underwent intensive training and the practical application of new tactical concepts. Because the minimum required height to be part of the battalion was 1.88 meters, members of this unit soon became known as Potsdam Giants, from the name of the city where their barracks were located. In 1713, the Red Battalion was attached to the Crown Prince Regiment, becoming its third battalion. The Crown Prince Regiment was then renamed the King's Regiment after the coronation of Frederick William I and continued to maintain the unusual establishment with three battalions and fifteen companies (all of grenadiers). The Red Grenadiers received higher pay and enjoyed several other privileges compared with the standard infantrymen from other regiments. The organizational reforms of Frederick William I affected the whole Prussian Army, but especially the various guard units. The Swiss Guard was abolished, while the Gendarmes were transformed into an ordinary cuirassier regiment after absorbing the Garde du Corps. The four regiments of Foot Guards had varying fortunes: the Leib-Garde Regiment was reduced to ten companies and lost its guard status (being

Musketeer (left), NCO (centre) and officer (right) of the Bataillon-Garde (1st Battalion of the 15th Infantry Regiment).

replaced by the King's Regiment in its bodyguard role), while the regiment of the Queen Consort (Dorothea of Brandenburg) also lost its guard denomination. The other two guard units remained unchanged. All these modifications took place in 1713, soon after the ascendancy of the new king. In 1716, the Weisse Grenadier-Garde lost its guard status too, after incorporating a large number of Swedish prisoners captured at the fall of Straslund.

Between 1713 and 1715, the Prussian line infantry was expanded with the creation of another seven regiments. The cavalry was then reformed in 1717 and 1718: all its units, be they heavy cavalry or dragoons, were now to be structured on five squadrons each. In 1704, two further regiments of dragoons had been formed, bringing the total number of dragoon units to six. One of these two new units was given guard status in 1714 and received the denomination of horse grenadiers. In 1717 and 1718, four of the existing dragoon regiments were transformed into units of cuirassiers, while two new regiments of dragoons were also created. Consequently, at the end of the Great Northern War, the Prussian Army comprised fourteen regiments of cuirassiers and four regiments of dragoons. In 1714, a company of pontoniers was added to the Artillery Corps, which in 1716 was restructured on two battalions (one of field artillery and one of garrison artillery). The Field Artillery Battalion was stationed in Berlin and had a total of five companies, while the Garrison Artillery Battalion had four companies that were scattered across the various fortresses of Prussia. Frederick William I died in 1740, and his son, Frederick II, became King of Prussia. By that time, the Prussian Army had undergone further organizational changes and consisted of the following units: one regiment of guard infantry, thirty regiments of infantry, four battalions of garrison infantry, twelve regiments of cuirassiers, seven regiments of dragoons, nine squadrons of hussars, one artillery battalion with six companies, four companies of garrison artillery and a small engineer corps consisting of just a few officers.

Chapter 3

The Wars of Frederick the Great

Frederick the Great ruled Prussia for a very long period, from 1740 until 1786. During these years, he revealed his military genius – which his father had not been able to see – and transformed the Kingdom of Prussia into the leading military power of Europe through the many victories of his army. Frederick knew that his realm was quite small compared with the major European countries of the time and that it had a modest population. As a result of this, following his accession to the Prussian throne in 1740 he tried to annex more territories to his kingdom. The main target of Frederick's expansionist policy was the region of Silesia, a German territory rich in important natural resources and having a large population, located south-east of Brandenburg. Silesia was part of the Holy Roman Empire but was not ruled as an autonomous princedom, being part of the many domains that were placed under the direct control of the Habsburg imperial family. The Habsburgs, as Holy Roman emperors, exerted nominal control over the entire territory of Germany, also dominating vast portions of Central Europe that made up their personal hereditary domains: Austria (the homeland of the Habsburgs), Styria, Carniola, Tyrol, Bohemia, Moravia, Silesia and Hungary, although the latter state was not formally part of the Holy Roman Empire. Following the end of the War of the Spanish Succession, the Habsburgs had also obtained other territories around Europe: the Austrian Netherlands (corresponding to present-day Belgium) and the Duchy of Milan in northern Italy.

The Habsburg Empire, or Austrian Empire, was extremely vast and rich, but had serious political problems that caused its relative military weakness. Some of its territories were greatly exposed to the attacks of rival powers, such as the Austrian Netherlands, which were constantly menaced by the expansionist ambitions of France. In the east, Hungary had a vast southern border with the Ottoman Empire, where a low-intensity war was fought between the Habsburgs and the Ottomans for most of the eighteenth century, which consumed a good deal of the Austrians' military resources. The German princedoms of the Holy Roman Empire mostly resented Habsburg rule and tried to augment their political autonomy in every possible way. Some German states, including Bavaria and Saxony, even had ambitions to take the place of Austria as the ruling power of the German world. Frederick was formally a

Grenadier (left), musketeer (centre left), officer (centre right) and NCO (right) of the Bataillon-Garde (1st Battalion of the 15th Infantry Regiment).

vassal of the Habsburgs because of his possession of Brandenburg, but he was also the only fully autonomous king in the Holy Roman Empire because Prussia was not part of the empire. The Habsburgs were Catholics and had been the strongest ally of the Papacy during the wars that had been fought against the Protestants in the previous two centuries; Prussia, instead, had assumed the role of protector of the German Protestants since the late seventeenth century. Frederick II's foreign policy was based on the idea that Prussia could only become the ruling power of the German world if Austria was defeated by the Prussian Army. As a result, Silesia was the natural target of Prussian expansionism, as by conquering it the Prussians would improve the economic capabilities of their state and while greatly weakening those of the Austrian Empire. Silesia had a great financial value as a source of tax revenue, but was also, by the standards of the time, a highly industrialized area of Central Europe. It had a large population from which substantial numbers of soldiers could be recruited, and was crossed by prosperous commercial routes. Additionally, Silesia had a significant geo-strategic importance, since one of its core areas was the valley of the Upper Oder, which formed a natural military conduit between Brandenburg, Bohemia and Moravia. Before the ascendancy of Frederick to the throne, Prussia already had existing claims on substantial portions of Silesia. These derived from an inheritance treaty that had been signed in 1537, according to which three of the many duchies that made up Silesia (Liegnits, Wohlau and Brieg) were to pass to Brandenburg if the independent dynasty of Silesia became extinct. The Habsburgs never recognized the legitimacy of the Prussian claims, mainly because Silesia had always been part of the Kingdom of Bohemia, which was one of their personal possessions.

When Frederick became King of Prussia in May 1740, the Habsburg Empire was experiencing serious political problems regarding the issue of the 'Pragmatic Sanction', a document enacted by Holy Roman Emperor Charles VI in 1713, according to which a woman could inherit the territorial possessions of the Habsburgs. As Charles VI did not have a male heir, he wanted to designate his eldest daughter, Maria Theresa, as his successor. The Pragmatic Sanction went against the ancient Salic Law – that had been respected within the Holy Roman Empire for centuries – according to which only a man could inherit lands and titles. Initially, while Charles VI and Austria were still strong, it was accepted by most of the European powers and by the German princedoms. However, when Charles died in 1740, France (the fiercest enemy of the Habsburgs) and the most important German states (including Bavaria and Saxony) rejected it as a document having no legitimate legal basis. Taking advantage of this international situation and of the formation of a strong anti-Austrian alliance, Frederick pressed Prussia's claims on Silesia after rejecting the Pragmatic Sanction, as other European powers had already done. Maria Theresa, after her father's death, experienced serious political and military difficulties: she was able to retain control over only the hereditary possessions of her family and not the whole Holy Roman Empire. Both Charles Albert of Bavaria and Frederick August II of Saxony, who wanted to have the imperial crown for themselves, fielded armies against the Habsburgs, together with France (which wanted to exploit the temporary Austrian weakness to annex more lands in the Austrian Netherlands and the Rhineland).

In Prussia, Frederick, fearing that the difficulties of the Habsburgs could soon come to an end with a victory on one of the various military fronts where their troops were deployed, decided to strike first with great rapidity. On 16 December 1740, without an official declaration of war, the Prussian Army moved across the southern frontier of Brandenburg into Silesia. The 27,000-strong Prussian force was much more numerous than the local Austrian garrison, which had only 8,000 men. The Austrians were left with no other choice than to retreat into a couple of fortresses without fighting; by the end of January 1741, the invaders had occupied almost the entire territory of Silesia, including its capital of Breslau. In March, an Austrian army of 20,000 soldiers entered Silesia from Moravia and tried to surprise the Prussian forces besieging the Habsburg fortress of Neisse. The Austrian relief force and the Prussian troops faced each other at the Battle of Mollwitz on 10 April, the first major pitched clash fought between the Austrians and the Prussians. Although the battle was indecisive, it halted the Austrian reconquest of Silesia. During the following months, the two sides temporarily suspended hostilities and opened negotiating. Meanwhile, the lands of the Habsburgs were coming under attack from all directions: a French army had crossed the Rhine and had joined the Bavarians in their advance towards Vienna, while a combined Spanish and Neapolitan force was attacking the Duchy of Milan in Italy. Maria Theresa, faced with the prospect of a total partition of her territorial possessions, travelled to Hungary, where she was able to win the loyalty of the local nobility and recruit a new army. In order to deal with the Saxon invasion of Bohemia, the Austrians had no choice but to sign a temporary truce with Frederick and to cede Silesia to Prussia. In the closing months of 1741, instead of advancing on Vienna, the Franco-Bavarian army moved to Bohemia, where it joined forces with the Saxons and occupied Prague on 26 November. At this point of the conflict, now known as the War of the Austrian Succession, Prussia decided to join with its allies in the invasion of Bohemia and Moravia, meaning an end to the Austro-Prussian truce. As a result of the allies obtaining a series of victories over Austria, Charles Albert of Bavaria was elected as the new Holy Roman Emperor in January 1742. During that year, however, cooperation among the anti-Austrian alliance ceased because of the allies' contrasting political ambitions. Saxony ended its participation in the war,

Grenadier of the 2nd Infantry Regiment (left) and grenadier of the 7th Infantry Regiment (right).

France did not advance on Vienna and Prussia achieved very little in Moravia. As a result of these events, the Habsburgs could assemble a new force of 30,000 soldiers to reconquer Bohemia. The Austrians and Prussians then clashed at the Battle of Chotusitz in Bohemia, which ended in hard-fought victory for Frederick's men.

After these events, the Prussians intensified their efforts to reach a separate peace with Austria. Negotiators from the two belligerents met in Breslau for peace talks. Initially, Maria Theresa had no intention of ceding the whole of Silesia to Prussia, since she knew that this would be a mortal blow for the economy of her empire. Eventually, however, she was obliged to accept Frederick's demands due to strong diplomatic pressure exerted by the British (who had provided large sums of money to the Austrians in order to sustain the war efforts of the Habsburgs). On 11 June 1742, the Treaty of Breslau was signed between Austria and Prussia, according to which the whole of Silesia – except for a very small portion of territory – was assigned to Frederick. In exchange for receiving this territorial concession, the Prussians promised to end their participation in the war and to leave the anti-Austrian alliance. Thus ended the First Silesian War between Austria and Prussia, although the War of the Austrian Succession continued for several more years. Frederick of Prussia, a young monarch with no previous experience, had been able to secure 35,000 square kilometres of new territory for his realm and to acquire around a million new subjects. With the Kingdom of Prussia removed from the wider war, Austria was able to launch major counter-attacks on all the other fronts and gradually regain the territorial possessions that it had lost between 1740 and 1742. While the Treaty of Breslau had cost the Habsburgs their richest province, it enabled them to save the rest of their empire. The annexation of Silesia transformed Prussia into a first-rate power within the Holy Roman Empire, since its military and economic capabilities were now comparable – if not superior – to those of well-established regional powers such as Bavaria and Saxony. Frederick's diplomatic betrayal of his allies in 1742, however, had important consequences for the international position of Prussia, as both France and Saxony became increasingly hostile towards the rising power of the Kingdom of Prussia.

In the summer of 1744, hoping to obtain more territories in Central Europe – and especially in Bohemia – Prussia broke the terms of the Treaty of Breslau and re-entered the War of the Austrian Succession against the Habsburgs. Frederick invaded Bohemia with an army of 70,000 men, divided into three separate columns. These quickly converged on Prague, which had been reconquered by the Habsburgs just a few months before, and laid siege to it. After a week of heavy artillery bombardment, the city, the capital of Bohemia, surrendered to Frederick on 16 September. Frederick soon after marched southwards, conquering further territories, but the Austrian response was swift and effective, a large army being sent against the Prussians in Bohemia, and Saxony being persuaded to re-enter the conflict against Prussia. Frederick tried to force a decisive pitched battle against the Austrians, but without success. He was thus forced to leave Prague and to retreat into Silesia, where he repulsed several Austrian

Officer (left) and musketeer (right) of the 5th Infantry Regiment.

incursions during the following winter. In April 1745, the Habsburgs obtained an important victory over the Franco-Bavarian forces at the Battle of Pfaffenhofen, after which they occupied most of Bavaria. At this point of the conflict, the Bavarians renounced their claims on the title of Holy Roman Emperor, which was now assigned to Maria Theresa's husband, Francis Stephen of Lorraine. Having made peace with the Bavarians, Austria prepared a large-scale invasion of Silesia, with the support of Saxony. On 4 June 1745, however, Frederick decisively defeated the joint Austro-Saxon military force at the Battle of Hohenfriedberg, thereby preventing the

Habsburgs from reconquering Silesia. It was following this victory that the Prussian monarch started to be called Frederick the Great. In November 1745, the Austrian and Saxon troops launched a fresh offensive against Prussian Silesia. The Prussians, however, defended their territories effectively, as they had done in the recent past. They destroyed a Saxon army at the Battle of Hennersdorf, forcing the Austrians to abandon Silesia. After these successes, a Prussian army was sent to invade Saxony and was able to occupy the strategically important cities of Leipzig and Dresden. At this point, both Maria Theresa and Frederick the Great recognized that there was no sense in continuing the war between their two countries. As a result, on 25 December 1745, the Second Silesian War came to an end with the signing of the Treaty of Dresden. According to this, Maria Theresa recognized Silesia as a province of Prussia, while Frederick recognized the validity of the Pragmatic Sanction as well as the imperial election of Francis Stephen of Lorraine. The larger War of the Austrian Succession, of which the two Silesian Wars had been part, ended only in 1748.

The years of peace that followed the end of the War of the Austrian Succession were extremely complex from a diplomatic point of view, since none of the major powers were satisfied with the peace agreements that had been reached in 1748. The Habsburgs were determined to reconquer Silesia as soon as possible, and were even disposed to ally themselves with some of their former enemies in order to achieve this objective. Understanding this, Frederick the Great strove to improve the fortifications of Silesia in the years that followed 1745 to protect against a future Austrian invasion. The Habsburgs spent the period from 1748–56 reforming their system of taxation, with the intention of having larger sums of money at their disposal that could be employed to expand the army. The Austrian army was professionalized and retrained following the Prussian model, and the whole administrative system of the Habsburg Empire was modernized. The Austrians also worked to break the international isolation of their country, opening negotiations with Russia and France. In 1746, Maria Theresa of Austria and Empress Elizabeth of Russia signed an anti-Prussian defensive pact. A few years later, Austrian and French diplomats began discussing the idea of creating an anti-Prussian alliance. The Kingdom of France had been the traditional rival of the Habsburgs since the sixteenth century, but the balance of power in Europe was now changing in a dramatic way. The ascendancy of Prussia in Central Europe worried both the Habsburgs of Austria and the Bourbons of France, who did not want to see the emergence of a new military power in the heart of the Continent. The negotiations between Austrian and French diplomats led to the Diplomatic Revolution of 1756, which saw the formation of a military alliance between the Habsburgs and the Bourbons. This dramatic change in the diplomatic status quo of Europe would have been unthinkable just a few years before, as the contrasting interests that divided Austria from France had always been extremely significant. Frederick the Great, however, had already understood that a new anti-Prussian alliance was in the process of being formed, and had anticipated his enemies by breaking the international isolation of his country.

On 16 January 1756, before the alliance between the Habsburgs and the Bourbons became official, Prussia signed the Westminster Convention with Great Britain. According to this treaty, the British would not support Austria in a renewed conflict for the possession of Silesia if the Prussians agreed to protect Hanover from France. At the time, the German state of Hanover was a possession of British monarch George II, whose family came from Hanover; as a result, Britain and the German princedom were ruled by the same monarch in 'personal union'. France had long wanted to invade Hanover and had attempted to do so in the past. Consequently, in order to have a strong ally on the Continent that could protect Hanoverian territory, the British government decided to form a new alliance with Frederick. In 1756 and 1757, two treaties of alliance were signed at Versailles between Austria and France; the first had a defensive nature, while the second was much more important since it effectively led to the formation of an offensive anti-Prussian alliance. The political changes resulting from the Diplomatic Revolution of 1756 were one of the key factors behind the outbreak of a new large-scale European conflict, the Seven Years' War, which began in August 1756 with a pre-emptive Prussian strike against Saxony. Frederick the Great was convinced, correctly, that his country would have been attacked by both Austria and Russia in early 1757. Before this could happen, he decided to launch an offensive against the most important German ally of the Austrians: Saxony. The Prussian plans for the forthcoming war showed great intelligence on their part. First of all, Frederick wanted to invade Saxony in order to absorb the Saxon military into his army and to use the Saxon treasury for his war efforts. After the occupation of Saxon lands, the Prussians planned to invade Bohemia and Moravia before advancing on Vienna in order to force an end to the conflict. Everything had to be done in more or less one year, before the Russians could send massive amounts of troops into Central Europe to help their Austrian allies. Britain was to support Frederick with substantial financial aid and by sending a naval squadron into the Baltic Sea to protect Prussia's coastline from incursions by the Russian navy. Frederick mobilized all his available forces for the new war and distributed them as follows: 28,000 soldiers were stationed in East Prussia and Farther Pomerania to protect them from a Russian invasion, 25,000 men were deployed in Silesia in order to face an eventual Austrian offensive, and 60,000 soldiers were to conduct the invasion of Saxony.

The Prussian invasion of Saxony began on 29 August 1756 and was a complete success, the Saxons having not been prepared to face a large-scale attack and thus

Drummer (left), officer (centre) and musketeer (right) of the 11th Infantry Regiment.

having not assembled their forces for a military campaign. On 9 September, the Saxon capital of Dresden was occupied by Frederick, who met very little resistance during his advance as the Saxons had decided to fortify themselves at Pirna and wait for the arrival of an Austrian relief army. Frederick the Great did not wait for the arrival of the Austrians, instead anticipating their move by invading Bohemia. The first major clash of the conflict – known as the Third Silesian War, part of the larger Seven Years' War – took place at Lobositz on 1 October. The Prussians won the battle from a strategic point of view, since they prevented the Austrians from marching towards Pirna to support the Saxons, but were not able to crush the Austrian forces facing

Officer (left) and musketeer (right) of the 18th Infantry Regiment. The musketeer is already wearing the tricorn shaped like a bicorn, which was introduced during the last years of Frederick the Great's rule.

them. On 14 October, after a brief siege, the Saxon Army at Pirna surrendered to the Prussians, and thus the whole of Saxony could be occupied by Frederick's forces. As Frederick had planned, it was possible for him to absorb the Saxon troops into his army and to empty the rich Saxon treasury. The winter of 1756/57 did not see significant military operations, but there were important diplomatic moves: Britain decided to support the Prussians in a more active way, while Maria Theresa was able to mobilize an army of 40,000 men from the German princedoms of the Holy Roman Empire for the war against Frederick. Meanwhile, the Kingdom of France joined the Habsburgs and agreed to provide an army of 129,000 soldiers, in exchange for receiving the rich territory of the Austrian Netherlands at the end of hostilities. Russia also joined the anti-Prussian alliance, with the ambition of conquering East Prussia and then exchanging it with the Polish-Lithuanian Commonwealth for control of Courland on the Baltic. The Russians, for the moment, sent an army of 80,000 men to support the Habsburgs. Austria also convinced the Kingdom of Sweden to attack Prussia, with the promise of giving back to the Swedes the territories that they had lost in Pomerania following the end of the Great Northern War. With Austria, France, Russia and Sweden determined to defeat Frederick the Great and to partition Prussian territory among themselves, the Seven Years' War would prove a very difficult test for the military genius of the Prussian monarch.

In the spring of 1757, the Prussians launched their invasion of Bohemia before massive numbers of French and Russian troops could come to the aid of Austria. The Austrians tried to stop the Prussian forces at the Battle of Reichenberg, but were defeated and thus could do nothing to prevent the Prussian advance on Prague. On 6 May, the Battle of Prague was fought, a major clash which ended in another bloody victory for the Prussians. Both sides suffered heavy casualties, but the Austrians were forced to fall back into the city, where they were besieged by the Prussians. In an attempt to save the Bohemian capital, Maria Theresa sent a relief army of 30,000 soldiers to the region. Frederick the Great was forced to move with most of his troops against the Austrian army, thus reducing the number of Prussian soldiers besieging Prague. A pitched battle between the Prussian invaders and the Austrian relief force took place at Kolin on 18 June and ended in a significant Habsburg victory, the numerical superiority of the Austrians having proved decisive. Frederick was forced to lift the siege of Prague and to leave Bohemia with all his forces. While these events took place in Bohemia, a Russian army of 75,000 men attacked East Prussia. Due to their great numerical inferiority, the Prussians had no choice but to retreat in good order and gain some time, in the hope that the Russians would halt their advance due to the overstretching of their supply lines. The Russian troops obtained some minor victories, but were eventually forced to stop in order to reorganize their forces, which were operating very far from home in a region inhabited by a hostile population. In the north-west, Sweden entered the conflict by invading Pomerania with 17,000 soldiers. For the moment, the Prussians could do very little to face the Swedes, and thus a good portion of Pomerania was occupied by them. During the summer of 1757, the Third Silesian War entered in its most important phase, a large army consisting of French troops as well as contingents from the German princedoms of the Holy Roman Empire entering the main theatre of operations from the west.

The anti-Prussian alliance had planned to reconquer Saxony as soon as possible, and for this reason both the Austrian troops operating in Bohemia and the Franco-German army coming from the west were converging towards Saxony. Frederick, determined to prevent the unification of the two main armies that were facing him, decided to move westwards across Thuringia to seek a decisive engagement with the approaching Franco-German forces. The following months were not easy for Prussia, since the Franco-German forces were able to avoid a direct confrontation with Frederick, while the Prussian capital of Berlin was briefly occupied by a small Hungarian cavalry force in Habsburg service. The French also occupied Hanover, which seemed to weaken the alliance between Prussia and Great Britain. On 5 November 1757, however, Frederick the Great was finally able to engage the large Franco-German army at the Battle of Rossbach, where, against all odds, the Prussians achieved an overwhelming victory, some 41,000 allied soldiers with 114 guns being soundly defeated by just 22,000 Prussians with 79 guns. The Franco-German force lost 10,000 men, the Prussians just 1,000. Once again, the Prussian Army had shown its superiority on the field of battle, being capable of defeating numerical advantage with discipline and training. After suffering such a costly and humiliating defeat, France soon withdrawn its remaining troops from the Silesian theatre of war and decided to avoid any future confrontation with the Prussians. While Frederick was fighting in Thuringia, an Austrian army invaded Silesia and defeated the local Prussian forces at the Battle of Breslau on 22 November. When Frederick heard of Breslau's fall, he and his 21,000 men marched 274 kilometres in just 12 days in order to join forces with the retreating Prussian troops that had been defeated at Breslau. Within a very short period, the Prussian king was able to assemble an army of 33,000 soldiers and march against the Austrians – mustering 66,000 men – who had camped around the village of Leuthen. On 5 December, despite the fact that his soldiers were extremely tired after their rapid march across Germany, and being badly outnumbered, Frederick the Great attacked the superior Habsburg forces at the Battle of Leuthen. As had happened just a month beforehand at Rossbach, the Prussians were able to prevail against a numerically superior enemy thanks to their iron discipline, training and morale. The Habsburg army suffered some 22,000 casualties, while Frederick's force lost less than a third of that number. After the victory at Leuthen, Prussian forces were able to rapidly reconquer Breslau and most of Silesia.

During the winter of 1757/58, Frederick hoped that Maria Theresa would decide to end the hostilities following the great Prussian victories of Rossbach and Leuthen. However, the Habsburgs continued their military and diplomatic efforts, aiming to retake control of Silesia. Taking advantage of the Austrian temporary weakness in the south and the Russian passivity in the east, Frederick the Great launched an offensive against the Swedes in Pomerania that was a great success and led to the Prussian blockade of Straslund. The Prussians also conducted a brilliant offensive against the French troops in Hanover, which drove the enemy out of the state and back to the western bank of the Rhine. The Prussian liberation of Hanover convinced the British that Frederick was still able to emerge victorious from the conflict and led to the arrival of fresh British financial aid for Prussia. On 11 April 1758, the British government formalized its new alliance with Prussia with the signing of the Anglo-Prussian Convention, according to which Great Britain committed to provide Prussia with an annual subsidy of £670,000 and to make no separate peace with any of Frederick the Great's enemies. At this point of the war, despite having been obliged to leave isolated East Prussia in the hands of the invading Russians, the Prussian monarch decided to invade Habsburg Moravia. The Austrians, still shocked by their defeat at Leuthen, preferred to avoid a direct confrontation with the Prussian Army, and instead focused on harassing enemy forces with their light troops recruited from the Balkans. This guerrilla war waged by the Austrians caused serious problems for the Prussians, who lost a massive supply convoy moving from Silesia to Moravia that was intercepted by the enemy. As a result, at risk of running out of supplies, Frederick had no choice but to suspend his invasion of Moravia. The Prussians returned to their home territories, where they fortified their defensive positions in Saxony and Silesia.

At this point of the Seven Years' War, after having underestimated them for a long time, Frederick the Great was forced to face the Russians on the north-eastern borders of his domains. The Russian Army, taking advantage of the scarcity of the Prussian forces opposing its advance, had been able to conquer large portions of Prussian territory during the previous months. The Russians had by now reached the borders of Brandenburg, from where they could move southwards to join forces with the Austrians. To avoid the danger of such a possibility, Frederick assembled an army of 35,000 men and moved against the Russians just east of the Oder River. Here, for the first time, the Russians – 43,000-strong – faced the Prussian monarch on the open field. During the ensuing Battle of Zorndorf, both sides fought to exhaustion and

Grenadier (left), musketeer (centre) and officer (right) of the 23rd Infantry Regiment.

suffered heavy casualties. Indeed, Frederick was surprised by the combat capabilities of the Russians, who put up a strong resistance against his Prussian veterans. Frederick could claim victory at the end of the battle as the Russians had abandoned the field, but in reality the clash at Zorndorf had been an indecisive affair. The autumn of 1758 saw the Prussians fighting against the Austrians in Saxony. Initially, both sides tried to avoid a major pitched clash, but the Prussian Army was eventually forced to fight by the Austrians and was defeated at the Battle of Hochkirch. This was one of the worst defeats suffered by Frederick the Great, who lost a good portion of his artillery and supplies in the encounter. Hochkirch, however, was just a temporary setback for the Prussians, who were able to regroup their forces and stop the Austrian advance into Saxony and Silesia. During the winter of 1758/59, the military situation did not change in any significant way, as the Russians retreated back to the Vistula River after having suffered serious losses at Zorndorf, while the Swedes launched a new attack against Pomerania but were repelled quite easily by the Prussians. In the south, Frederick remained in control of both Saxony and Silesia thanks to the new defences that he had organized in recent months.

In April 1759, with the resumption of military operations, Frederick moved his main army from Saxony into Silesia in order to keep the Russian troops deployed in western Poland separated from the Austrian forces stationed in Bohemia. The Russians, however, now had a more aggressive attitude since they had learned from experience that their troops could face the Prussians on almost equal terms. On 23 July, at the Battle of Kay, the Russian Army obtained a significant victory over the small Prussian forces opposing them, as a result of which Frederick the Great was forced to leave Silesia and move with most of his troops against the Russians. On 3 August, the Russian Army reached and occupied Frankfurt an der Oder, where it met with substantial reinforcements sent by the Austrians. Frederick had not been able to prevent what he feared most, as a new Austro-Russian army had just been formed not far from the heartland of Silesia. Determined to drive back his enemies, who were now within 80 kilometres of Berlin, the Prussian king assembled all available forces and decided to attack the Austro-Russian army around the village of Kunesdorf. On 12 August 1759, the Battle of Kunesdorf – one of the largest pitched clashes fought on European soil during the eighteenth century – took place, with the Austro-Russian army of 60,000 men facing Frederick's 50,000 Prussians. In the ensuing clash, Frederick was utterly defeated on the open field for the first time: his army suffered 20,000 casualties and lost most of its guns, disintegrating into an undisciplined mass. The battle was largely won by the allies due to their numerical superiority, but the general quality of the Austrian and Russian troops had also greatly improved, following the Prussian model. After the worst defeat in his long military

Officer (left) and musketeer (right) of the 24th Infantry Regiment.

career, Frederick tried to regroup what remained of his military forces to face a feared invasion of Prussia. His catastrophic expectations, however, did not become reality, due in the main to the internal divisions existing among his enemies. The Russians refused to invade Prussia immediately after the Battle of Kunesdorf, preferring to reorganize their forces, although the Austrians were eager to march on Berlin as soon as possible in order to defeat the Prussians once and for all. In September, despite their overwhelming superiority in Brandenburg, both the Russians and the Austrians decided to withdraw into Silesia in order to consolidate their positions. Prussia had been saved by some lucky circumstances, in what Frederick later termed as the 'Miracle of the House of Brandenburg'.

In early September 1759, the Austrian army pressed into Saxony from Bohemia, retaking Dresden and most of the Saxon lands without fighting any major clash with the Prussians. However, the Prussians were quickly able to reorganize themselves and obtain some minor victories over the Austrians. This convinced the Habsburgs to send most of their troops to Saxony to reinforce their newly established positions, while the Russians went back to Poland for the winter months. In this delicate phase of the conflict, Frederick the Great needed time more than anything else; he had to rebuild his military forces almost from scratch for future campaigns, which would prove decisive in determining the outcome of the war. In order to gain some time, he sent a single corps of his army to Maxen with orders to harass the Austrian lines of communication connecting Saxony with Bohemia. On 21 November, at the Battle of Maxen, this Prussian corps was defeated by the Austrians and forced to surrender; but this local setback gave some weeks of precious time to Frederick in the north. In the early months of 1760, the Prussian monarch could finally take the initiative once more against his enemies, who now consisted of two large armies (one operating in Silesia and another in Saxony). Frederick, against the expectations of the Habsburgs, decided to strike in Saxony and not to attempt a reconquest of Silesia. On 21 July 1760, the Prussians besieged Dresden, while the Austrians took the initiative in Silesia. The Austrians, determined to defeat the Prussians while they were still relatively weak, moved with their two armies against Frederick, but made the fatal mistake of attacking it separately. On 15 August, the Prussians defeated the first Austrian army at the Battle of Liegnitz, thanks to which they could reconquer a good portion of Silesia. The second Austrian army, which had been unable to join forces in time with the first one, went back to Saxony. In early October, the Russians launched a fresh offensive against Brandenburg, which met with success and led to their temporary occupation of Berlin. However, the overstretching of their supply lines obliged the Russians to suspend their occupation of Brandenburg before it could become a permanent one. As a result, Frederick could remain in the south to campaign against the Austrians. On 3 November, a large pitched battle was fought between the Prussians and the Austrians at Torgau. Despite being very costly for both sides, it was not a decisive clash, the Prussians claiming victory but being so badly weakened that they soon had to retreat to their winter quarters.

Officer of the 26th Infantry Regiment.

The Battle of Torgau left the war-making capacities of both the Prussians and the Austrians so depleted that neither side had any realistic prospect of bringing the hostilities to a successful close without receiving some decisive support from a third power. By the beginning of 1761, the Prussian Army could mostly field only units consisting of inexperienced raw recruits and suffered from a series of chronic shortages (for example, there were few muskets left for the infantry). The Austrians, meanwhile, were experiencing a state of chaos in their finances, with their economy choked by the heavy war taxes that were needed to continue the war. Cooperation between the Austrians and the Russians was breaking down, the two allies having developed contrasting interests and no longer being willing to fight costly pitched battles without having a clear political objective. During the summer of 1761, the main theatre of operations was in the north, where the Russians besieged and blockaded the Prussian port of Kolberg in Pomerania. Frederick, fearing that a Russian army could invade Brandenburg again and occupy Berlin, finally decided to abandon Kolberg and concentrate his troops for the defence of his capital. The fall of Kolberg, the last Baltic port of Prussia still in Frederick the Great's hands, had extremely negative consequences for the Prussians, as it denied them the possibility of receiving supplies from Great Britain. After transforming Kolberg into their main logistical base on the Baltic, the Russians prepared themselves for a decisive offensive against Berlin that would destroy once and for all the remaining Prussian military resources. On 5 January 1762, however, the Russian Empress Elizabeth died and was succeeded by her nephew, Peter. Elizabeth had been a strong supporter of the necessity to fight against the Prussians on Maria Theresa's side, but the new Tsar Peter III was an ardent admirer of Frederick the Great and came from the German Duchy of Holstein.

The new German monarch of Russia soon reversed the foreign policy of his country, ordering a ceasefire with Prussia. This unexpected decision was perceived as a 'Second Miracle of the House of Brandenburg' by Frederick, who quickly agreed an armistice with Russia. On 15 May 1762, the Treaty of Saint Petersburg was signed between Prussia and Russia, according to which the status quo existing on the border that separated Prussia from Russia was completely restored. After making peace with Russia, Frederick did the same with Sweden, with the pre-war situation restored in Pomerania. In the west, the Kingdom of France was exhausted too, after having been soundly defeated by Britain during the colonial campaigns that were fought in Canada and in India. Consequently, the French also ordered a ceasefire with Prussia. With his flanks now secured, Frederick could concentrate all his forces against the Austrians. He launched an invasion of Silesia that culminated in the Prussian victory at the Battle of Burkersdorf on 21 July 1762. Following this success, the Prussians could finally reconquer the whole of Silesia. During the closing months of 1762, Frederick also took the initiative in Saxony, where he defeated the Austrians at the Battle of Freiberg and could retake most of the country. In November, seeing that her state was on the verge of bankrupt, Maria Theresa proposed to open peace negotiations. Frederick agreed immediately, and on 24 November the two belligerents declared an armistice in Saxony and Silesia. The ensuing peace talks were extremely complex, since neither side had any intention of relinquishing the territories they had occupied during the conflict. Furthermore, Prussia had lost a good portion of its manpower, while Austria was facing a severe financial crisis. These factors favoured the positive conclusion of the negotiations, which culminated with the signing of the Treaty of Hubertusburg on 15 February 1763. According to the treaty's terms, Prussia retained possession of Silesia and Saxony was restored as an independent country. Frederick, however, was not obliged to pay any reparation for his lengthy occupation of Saxon lands during the conflict. In practice, the pre-war situation was restored, as if the Third Silesian War had never been fought. The Habsburgs made a further concession by formally renouncing their claims over Silesia, in return for which Frederick committed to support Maria Theresa's son – Archduke Joseph

Musketeer of the 26th Infantry Regiment.

– in the forthcoming Imperial Election of 1764. The Seven Years' War had ended in Central Europe.

However, the long and incredible military career of Frederick the Great did not end with the Seven Years' War, as during the later years of his reign he fought a further war against Austria. This, largely unknown today, was the War of the Bavarian Succession, originating from a Bavarian succession crisis. On 30 December 1777, the ruling Duke of Bavaria, Max Joseph, died of smallpox without direct heirs. Joseph I, Holy Roman Emperor since 1764 and co-ruler of the Austrian Empire together with his mother, Maria Theresa, coveted Bavaria, which was one of the richest princedoms that made up the Holy Roman Empire and had a long border with Austria. In addition, Bavaria was inhabited by a Catholic population that had many elements in common with the Austrians. Joseph I had married Max Joseph's sister in 1765, hoping that in the future he could claim the Duchy of Bavaria for his offspring. The marriage, however, lasted for just two years and thus did not provide Joseph with a strong legal claim when Max Joseph died in 1777. According to the dynastic laws that governed successions in the Holy Roman Empire, the Duchy of Bavaria would have been inherited by a minor branch of the Wittelsbach family. The Wittelsbach family governed Bavaria with its major branch and the Palatinate with its minor branch; since the Bavarian branch did not have an heir for the deceased Max Joseph, the Duchy of Bavaria would have been inherited by Charles Theodore of the Palatinate (the leading member of the Wittelsbach family's minor branch). As both the Count of the Palatinate and Duke of Bavaria were among the German nobles who participated in the election of the Holy Roman Emperor, dynastic laws prohibited the formation of a 'personal union' between the Palatinate and Bavaria. As a result, if he wanted to become Duke of Bavaria, Charles Theodore would have been obliged to resign as Count of the Palatinate.

Charles Theodore was supported in the succession process by Joseph I, with whom he concluded a treaty according to which some areas of Lower Bavaria would be assigned to Austria. Frederick the Great of Prussia supported a different pretender in order to avoid the possibility that Bavaria could come under the direct political influence of the Habsburgs. Frederick's pretender was Charles II August, heir presumptive of the deceased Max Joseph. Charles Theodore was supported not only by Austria but also by France, the Habsburgs and Bourbons having confirmed their alliance in the years that followed the end of the Seven Years' War with the marriage between Maria Theresa's daughter, Marie Antoinette, and the future King of France, Louis XVI. Charles Theodore, counting on the loyalty of his new subjects, was able to assume control over Bavaria, soon after which, according to the pact he had signed with Joseph I, Austrian troops occupied a portion of Lower Bavaria. Following these events, a diplomatic crisis broke out between Austria and Prussia since Frederick the Great considered the partial occupation of Bavaria by the Habsburgs as unacceptable. The Prussian Army was mobilized, while Joseph I tried to obtain some concrete support from the French. The latter, however, were fighting against Britain in the American Revolution and thus could not participate in a large-scale European conflict. Frederick, despite not being able to count on the financial support of his old British allies, had the support of Saxony. After some months of failed negotiations, hostilities broke out between the Austrian Empire and the Kingdom of Prussia in the spring of 1778. The Prussian Army attacked first, striking in Bohemia, but after some initial progress it was forced to halt, confronted by the new lines of defence that had been established by the Habsburgs in Bohemia during the previous decades. These defences were impressive for the standards of the time, mounting a large number of guns; taking them would have caused severe losses to the Prussians. As a consequence, the war soon entered into a stalemate, the Prussians declining to launch a major offensive and the Austrians limiting themselves to conducting some hit and run incursions with their light troops. The soldiers of both sides spent most of their time foraging for food rather than fighting, leading to the War of the Bavarian Succession being commonly

Officer of the 27th Infantry Regiment.

known as the Potato War in Germany since most of its casualties derived from starvation and not from actual fighting. Four separate armies – two Austrian and two Prussian – faced each other for several months without conducting major actions.

Frederick, recognizing the strength of the enemy defences in Bohemia, was not disposed to lose many of his precious soldiers just to have his candidate on the Bavarian throne. Furthermore, he was worried that his realm could be attacked by Russia or Sweden while most of the Prussian Army was facing the Austrians in the south. The Habsburg family was divided on how to resolve the diplomatic and military crisis: Joseph I was ready to fight a pitched battle against Frederick the Great in order to gain some personal military glory, but Maria Theresa organized secret peace negotiations soon after the hostilities began. When the Holy Roman Emperor discovered his mother's manoeuvring behind his back, he was furious; in the end, however, he was forced to accept the mediation of Catherine of Russia, a move sponsored by Maria Theresa and accepted by Frederick the Great. The four armies deployed along the Bohemian border went back to their winter quarters, leaving just a few cavalry units in the area. During the early months of 1779, while peace talks were taking place, the Austrians launched several medium-scale incursions against the Prussians in southern Silesia that obtained some successes. The conflict, however, did not see a new escalation, since both sides were by now determined to find a diplomatic solution. This was reached with the signing of the Treaty of Teschen in May 1779, according to which the Habsburgs returned the territories they had occupied in Bavaria to Charles Theodore. Prussia, meanwhile, officially recognized Charles Theodore as the legitimate Duke of Bavaria. A few years after the end of the War of the Bavarian Succession, both Frederick the Great and Maria Theresa – who had initiated their reigns in 1740 by fighting against each other in the First Silesian War – died. Maria Theresa died in 1780 and was succeeded by her son, Joseph I, while Frederick died in 1786 and was succeeded by the eldest son of his younger brother – who ruled as Frederick William II – since he had no direct heirs.

Chapter 4
The Infantry

History and Organization

The well-disciplined and perfectly drilled infantry made up the backbone of Frederick the Great's Prussian Army. They were recruited according to the Canton System described in a previous chapter, and thus their excellent quality was mostly the result of Frederick William I's innovative military reforms. Frederick did not change the overall organization of his army's infantry during his long reign, as the regiments that he inherited from his father were already excellent in every aspect. However, he constantly expanded his foot troops, as he did with the rest of his army. When he became king in 1740, the Prussian forces numbered around 83,000 soldiers; by the time of the War of the Bavarian Succession in 1777, the Prussian Army had in the region of 190,000 men. Frederick the Great continued the militarization of his realm that had been initiated by Frederick William I: every Prussian man became a soldier and the whole of Prussian society was dominated by militaristic ideals. The nobility played a prominent role in this process, since the *junkers* commanded the great majority of the army's regiments. Numerical expansion, which was the result of Frederick's conquest of Silesia as well as the need for more troops to defend Prussian territories from the attacks of multiple enemies, was not easy to achieve for a state such as the Kingdom of Prussia, which had only around five million inhabitants. During the bloody Seven Years' War, Prussian armies were annihilated on several occasions, meaning that Frederick the Great had to rebuild his military almost from scratch more than once. He was able to do so thanks to the effective recruiting system that he inherited from his father, but this had enormous financial and social costs. By 1763, the Prussian state had used all the available manpower and could no longer sustain a large-scale war mobilization. Rebuilding the destroyed regiments by recruiting new soldiers in the various cantons imposed enormous sacrifices on the peasant families, which represented the core of Prussian society because Frederick the Great's state had an economy based on agriculture. From a qualitative point of view, the best troops commanded by Frederick were those that took part in the First Silesian War and the first part of the Third Silesian War, since they consisted of soldiers who had undergone the full training programme of

Musketeer of the 27th Infantry Regiment.

the Prussian Army. The new regiments raised during the Third Silesian War, instead, consisted of raw recruits who had very little combat experience and were considered as expendable by their king. Numerical expansion, as frequently happens in military matters, did not correspond to an increase in quality. Nevertheless, Frederick was at war with almost all the great European powers and thus had no choice but to mobilize every able-bodied man of his realm. The prevention of desertion, which could be a plague for an army made up of non-professional soldiers like that of Frederick the Great, necessitated a level of discipline that was regarded as savage even by military standards of the time. The Prussian monarch was strongly convinced that his army could be prevented from breaking up only by employing draconian measures, including physical beatings by NCOs, branding, running the gauntlet and executions. A Prussian soldier thus usually feared his superiors more than his enemies. The great majority of the Prussian Army's officers were aristocrats, who had either been trained in the cadet school of Berlin or had joined their regiments as aspirant officers in order to learn their job from experience. They were responsible for keeping a high level of brutality in the discipline of their men and for supervising training with great attention.

The infantry of the Prussian Army was trained to fight in close order and to advance in line to maximize firepower.

The flintlock muskets of the eighteenth century were accurate only at very short distances, which meant that bayonet charges were often much more decisive for the outcome of a clash than musket volleys. When required to do so, Prussian infantrymen could manoeuvre in a succession of lines in order to form an open column. In all their tactical formations, the files were closed up very tightly, with each man's right arm positioned behind his neighbour's left arm. Frederick the Great inherited a four-rank line from his father, which he immediately amended to three ranks in 1740. Shortages of manpower experienced during the Seven Years' War obliged the Prussian king to use two-deep ranks on several occasions, but this never became the rule. Manoeuvring was conducted in open columns of platoons, with a frontage of between twenty and twenty-five paces and an interval between platoons sufficient to allow each of them to wheel and form a line of battle at a right angle to the line of approach. Frederick, especially during the first phase of his career, preferred employing his infantry to approach parallel to the enemy before wheeling to face them. Alternatively, the infantrymen could approach at right angles and then move obliquely to form a line in front of the enemy. Oblique manoeuvres were very difficult to perform on the field of battle, especially under enemy fire: it needed a lot of training and discipline to be conducted effectively. Such a movement was commonly known as a sloping march or traversing step, in which the following leg crossed over the leading leg. Since raw recruits were not capable of conducting oblique manoeuvring in this traditional manner, Frederick usually accomplished it during the Seven Years' War by simply facing the sub-units of each platoon to the right or left and having them march to a position that corresponded to their intended post in the line before having them face their front towards the enemy. Compared to the foot soldiers of other European armies of the time, a Prussian infantryman was capable of firing much more rapidly: up to four rounds per minute, the result of intensive training. Both loading and firing could be performed on the move, something that only experienced soldiers could do. Platoon fire produced a rolling volley along a unit's front, with each platoon firing in succession so that a fusillade was always coming from one section of the line. During the War of the Austrian Succession, Frederick often employed his infantry to conduct rapid bayonet assaults, since he was convinced that this could be much more decisive than protracted fire-fights taking place at short distance. Over time, however, he came to understand that the firepower of his infantrymen was superior to that of his opponents, which meant his troops suffered fewer casualties. Frederick was a great tactician and his favoured battle tactic was the oblique order, which permitted him to conceal his main manoeuvres while a small advance guard occupied the enemy's attention. Thanks to the use of the oblique order, the Prussian monarch could concentrate his troops upon one of the enemy's wings without being

Officer of the 28th Infantry Regiment.

seen and then more easily open a gap in the front of his opponents. Obtaining local superiority in a precise sector of the battlefield was fundamental for the Prussian infantry, which was usually outnumbered by its enemies during the pitched battles fought by Frederick the Great. The oblique order also had the advantage of allowing defeated units to withdraw in good order if needed, which was extremely important to save entire regiments from complete destruction. Only the Prussians were capable of conducting oblique manoeuvring under heavy fire delivered by their enemy, which proved a key factor in many of Frederick's stunning victories.

When Frederick II became King of Prussia in 1740, his infantry comprised one regiment with guard status: the famous King's Regiment created by his father, Frederick William I. One of this corps' nicknames was the Giant Guard of Potsdam, and its members were known as *Lange Kerle*, or Long Fellows, due to the height requirement of 1.88 metres to become part of the regiment. Frederick William I had an obsession with tall soldiers, wanting to create the most impressive guard regiment in Europe. He tried to obtain extra-tall recruits for his elite regiment by any means, including by recruiting them from the armies of other countries. The Emperor of Austria, Tsar of Russia and even the Ottoman Sultan sent him tall soldiers in order to encourage friendly relations between their countries and the Kingdom of Prussia. The King's

Regiment thus started to comprise an increasing number of giants, whose stature was – in several cases – the result of health problems. The eccentric and bizarre nature of the corps became apparent, especially when the Prussian monarch started to pay his agents deployed across Europe to kidnap giants who could become members of the regiment. Consequently, by the end of Frederick William I's reign, the Giant Guard of Potsdam was a largely useless unit from a military point of view since it was used only for parades on special occasions. Keeping in service such an extravagant corps, dressed in elegant uniforms, was extremely costly, especially because by 1740 it comprised three battalions, each with seven companies. The tallest individuals of the regiment marched in the front line of their unit during parades and were the object of special attentions from Frederick William I. When one of them – a former Norwegian blacksmith named Jonas – died, the king had him reproduced in marble. The Prussian monarch even tried to pair his giant soldiers with tall women, in order to breed new giants who could become members of his guard. At that time, gigantism was not considered a serious health problem, and the life of these unlucky soldiers coming from every corner of Europe was not particularly happy. Frederick William I trained and drilled them every day; he even liked to paint their portraits and to show them to the foreign dignitaries who visited his royal palace. The Long Fellows also had a regimental mascot, an extremely tall bear. Their uniform was the most ornate and costly of the whole Prussian Army. When Frederick became king in 1740, he soon turned his attention to the corps, which he considered an unnecessary expense. Indeed, with the sums of money that were spent to keep the Giant Guard of Potsdam in service, the Prussian Army could maintain eight regiments of standard infantry. The new monarch soon reduced the unit to the establishment of a single battalion, which continued to perform only parade duties. Known as the Grenadier-Garde Battalion, it retained its usual uniform and equipment in memory of Frederick William I and even continued to bear the latter's cypher on its colours. A new unit of normal infantry was formed to replace the two disbanded battalions of the King's Regiment, being numbered the 6th Regiment of the Prussian infantry. While still a prince, according to a well-established Prussian military tradition, Frederick the Great had commanded the 15th Infantry Regiment as his personal unit. As a result, after he became king, the regiment was given guard status and took the place of the Giant Guard of Potsdam. Differently from the latter, however, the new guard regiment did participate in several combat actions. It was structured on four battalions: the 1st Battalion, also known as the Leib-Garde or Bataillon-Garde, was the most prestigious corps of the Prussian infantry. It acted as a ceremonial corps stationed at Potsdam and its parade performances were unsurpassed in Europe. The 2nd Battalion and 3rd Battalion were assembled together to form a separate elite combat unit that took part

Musketeer of the 28th Infantry Regiment.

with distinction in all the major campaigns fought by Frederick the Great. The fourth battalion was a depot unit and did not have a number; for this reason it was known as the Corps der Unrangirten (Unregimented/Unnumbered Corps). It acted as the training school for the whole Prussian infantry and thus – despite not participating in pitched battles itself – played a very important role in the Prussian Army.

Each of the infantry regiments of the Prussian Army comprised two battalions, apart from the guard infantry regiment described above and the 3rd Infantry Regiment that had three battalions. The regiment was the principal administrative unit of the armies of the time and was – to a large extent – the property of the colonel-in-chief who recruited it. The colonel-in-chief was a *junker* from one of Prussia's most important noble families, who was responsible for the administration and finances of his unit. Actual command of each regiment was assigned to a colonel-commandant, who was responsible for leading the unit in battle. The influence of the colonel-in-chief over his regiment was so important that the unit was usually named after him, although each regiment of the Prussian infantry also had a progressive number. The infantry regiments could in some respects be considered as a family possession, since they could be administered by the same noble family for several generations. Each colonel-commandant, who usually had the rank of lieutenant colonel while his colonel-in-chief had the rank of general, was aided by two majors. Each major commanded a battalion, which consisted of six companies: five of musketeers and one of grenadiers. Musketeers were the standard line infantrymen, while grenadiers were elite infantry tasked with performing specific duties. Grenadiers emerged as a new troop type of European infantry during the second half of the seventeenth century, when the various armies started to employ hand grenades as a new weapon. Grenades could be thrown by infantrymen and were quite simple to produce, and furthermore they could be of great use during siege operations and could also be employed during pitched battles to destroy enemy field fortifications. In order to use this new weapon most effectively, the infantry units of the European armies started to select the tallest and strongest men among their members, who were retrained as grenadiers and learned how to use hand grenades on the battlefield. This development took place during the second half of the seventeenth century, when the dominant military power of Europe was the Kingdom of France. Ruled by the 'Sun King', Louis XIV, France had at its disposal the most innovative military force of the age. The French Army was the first to create independent units of grenadiers within the infantry regiments. From 1667, four men in each French infantry regiment started to be trained as grenadiers, and in 1671 a company of grenadiers was included in each infantry battalion. During the following decades, grenadiers became the elite of the French foot troops, thanks to their superior training and discipline. As time progressed, the French innovations were adopted by the other European armies, meaning grenadiers could be found practically everywhere in the Continent.

The musketeer companies of the Prussian infantry regiments had the following internal establishment: one captain, one first lieutenant, one or two second lieutenants, one ensign, sixteen NCOs and 114 privates. In addition to the above, there were various supernumeraries who were generally released from service in time of peace. In January 1757, the number of privates in each company was increased to 144, but this figure was rarely reached during the course of the Seven Years' War due to the shortage of manpower that affected the Prussian Army. The grenadier companies, meanwhile, had a very similar internal establishment: one captain, one first lieutenant, one or two second lieutenants, one ensign, sixteen NCOs and 144 privates. Each Prussian infantry regiment had its own staff, which comprised the following elements: one provost officer, two quartermasters, one chaplain, one medical officer, twelve medical assistants, one drum-major, fifty musicians (thirty-eight drummers, six fifers and six oboists), twelve pioneers and a variable number of craftsmen (gunsmiths and armourers). The pioneers, one for each company, played a very important operational role, being assigned the tasks of a modern combat engineer, capable of building field fortifications. Each musketeer company had a medical assistant and five musicians (three drummers, one fifer and one oboist), who were tasked with transmitting orders and with guiding the movements of the foot soldiers with their music. The captain, or Hauptmann, was responsible for the entire administration of his company and received money from the colonel-in-chief to cover pay, maintenance and supply of the individual equipment needed by his men.

Each regiment comprised a Leib (or Life) Company, which was the senior company of the unit; this had an elite status and had as honorary commander the colonel-in-chief. The administration of the Leib Company was entrusted to an officer known as a Stabskapitan, or staff captain, who was actually a lieutenant. The commissioned ranks below captain, as we have already seen, were lieutenant and ensign; the latter, despite its denomination, was not a colour-bearer, since the colour of each regiment was usually carried by an experienced NCO. The Prussian infantry had a dual system of NCO appointment: the veteran NCOs promoted from the ranks included corporal, sergeant and sergeant major, while the lowest rank, lance corporal, was not a true NCO but rather an experienced private. There was also a parallel organization of aspirant officers or cadets, who had to learn in the field before being given officer commissions. These, known as Freikorporals – or free corporals – performed NCO duties and could be given the honour of carrying the standard of their regiment. From a tactical point of view, each infantry battalion was subdivided into eight platoons, with two platoons making up a division. Since

Officer of the 29th Infantry Regiment.

the four divisions could not be divided equally into the five musketeer companies of each battalion, it was necessary for the men to be separated from their companies and then reassigned into the eight platoons. The grenadier companies did not normally serve with the remainder of their regiment, since on active service they were assembled together to form composite grenadier battalions. These had a temporary nature and were mostly employed to perform special missions; they usually consisted of four grenadier companies from two different infantry regiments. In the Prussian infantry, differently from what happened in other European armies, grenadiers were not selected for their height but for their stalwart character and previous combat experience. The establishment with four companies of a grenadier battalion coincided with the tactical organization, since each company formed one division with two platoons.

In addition to the grenadier battalions described above, Frederick the Great could also count on six permanent independent units of grenadiers. These, known as standing grenadier battalions, were created by Frederick, with two of them raised during the Second Silesian War and another four after the end of the conflict. The standing grenadier battalions, comprising six companies each, were created by assembling the grenadier companies of the garrison infantry regiments. The latter were tasked with guarding the fortresses of Brandenburg-Prussia and thus were static foot units that made up a reserve. When Frederick became king, the Prussian infantry comprised just four garrison infantry regiments, made up of men who were no longer regarded as capable of performing field service. Two of these battalions were stationed in East Prussia, one in Pomerania and one at Magdeburg. The new monarch soon expanded his garrison troops to an establishment of twelve regiments, each of which could have from a minimum of two to a maximum of four battalions. Each battalion usually consisted of five musketeer companies, since Frederick the Great used the grenadier companies of the Garrison Infantry Battalions to form the new standing grenadier battalions. During the Seven Years' War, the shortage of personnel became so acute for the Prussian infantry that some garrison infantry regiments were mobilized for field duty. Their battalions were attached as additional battalions to the units of active infantry and performed well enough on the battlefield. In addition to the garrison infantry regiments, the Prussian infantry also included the new garrison infantry regiments that were later given the denomination of land infantry regiments or territorial infantry regiments. These, organized in 1742, were raised only in wartime from old veterans and impressed young peasants. There were a total of five of them, garrisoned in the major urban centres of Brandenburg-Prussia. In 1757, during the worst moments of the military crisis that invested the Prussian Army, Frederick ordered the raising of twenty-two militia battalions from the eastern areas of his realm that were being invaded by the Russians. These, which proved to be of very little military use, were all disbanded at the end of the hostilities.

When Frederick became king in 1740, the Prussian infantry had thirty regiments of infantry, a number increased to thirty-eight upon the outbreak of the First Silesian War. Another three regiments were added in 1741, followed by one more in 1742. A further four regiments were added to the general establishment of the Prussian infantry in 1743, bringing the total number to forty-six. Several of the new units included a high percentage of non-Prussian soldiers who came into Prussian service after having been raised for the armies of other German states. Of the sixteen new infantry regiments created by Frederick the Great during the War of the Austrian Succession, fourteen received the official denomination of fusilier regiment, since their members – being foreigners or coming from newly conquered Silesia – were of smaller physical stature than the Prussian soldiers who made up the thirty original musketeer regiments. A fusilier regiment was different from a musketeer regiment in just for two aspects: its members were equipped with a shorter version of the standard infantry musket and wore the metal-fronted cap of grenadiers (which was used only by the grenadier companies in a musketeer regiment). The original thirty regiments of the Prussian infantry, being recruited according to the Canton System, had a distinct regional identity; the single guard regiment, did not have this, since it was recruited from the best elements of the standard infantry units. The new fusilier regiments, including large numbers of foreigners, were not linked to any particular area of Brandenburg-Prussia. During the Seven Years' War, the Prussian infantry was expanded with the addition of another two regiments: the first was raised in 1756, while the second – obtained by converting a regiment of pioneers – was formed in 1758. During the early months of the Third Silesian War, Frederick the Great invaded Saxony and absorbed the state's military forces into the Prussian Army. As a result of this, in October 1756, ten infantry regiments made up of Saxon soldiers were added to the establishment of the Prussian Army. These units, however, had a very short existence, since most of their members deserted a few months after becoming part of the Prussian infantry. Seven of the original ten regiments were disbanded; the remaining three were retained in service until 1763. During 1773 and 1774, Frederick the Great carried out the last expansion of his infantry, creating six new regiments, meaning that by the time he died in 1786, the Prussian Army had fifty-four infantry regiments.

During the opening decades of the eighteenth century, line infantry was the most important component of European armies, making up the bulk of the troops mobilized by the various nations and having acquired tactical superiority over cavalry. Highly trained and well-disciplined, it consisted of musketeers able to march and manoeuvre

Musketeer of the 29th Infantry Regiment.

in perfect order by maintaining shoulder-to-shoulder close formations. While moving on the battlefield, the line infantrymen advanced in columns; when stopping to open fire upon the enemy, they were deployed into long lines. After some rolling volleys of musketry were exchanged between the two opposing infantry formations, a clash could continue in two different ways: on most occasions, one of the two lines was shattered by the enemy fire and decided to retreat (usually keeping order among the ranks and readopting column formation); but occasionally it was necessary to fight hand-to-hand with bayonets to determine the outcome of the confrontation. Keeping order in the formations and delivering a regular fire were the key factors behind victory, meaning training was decisive in transforming line infantry into an effective tactical tool. Generally speaking, battles were extremely static, since maintaining perfect order in the formations obliged the infantrymen to move very slowly. The transition from the column formation to the line was extremely delicate, as it exposed the infantry to the sudden charges of cavalry. When confronting mounted troops, line infantry usually adopted a standard defensive formation known as the square: this was another kind of close order, created many years ago with the aim of stopping enemy attacks by using the bayonets as pikes against men on horseback.

The formations and tactics described above were determined by the performances of the muskets that were used during the eighteenth century. These were flintlock weapons, whose loading operations were quite complicated. This meant that only one or two musket balls were shot in a minute, considering the standard performance of a line infantryman with acceptable training. The flintlock muskets of the period were all smoothbores and thus extremely inaccurate. When a ball was fired, it came out from the weapon without a precise direction, since there were no grooves inside the barrel that could guide it. A flintlock musket was of use only when fired at 100–200 metres from the target, so during a battle, the line infantry formations had to come very close together in order to use their weapons with some degree of effectiveness. The muskets of the age were also extremely heavy, which greatly limited the mobility of the foot soldiers. When moving on broken terrain, for example covered with rocks or trees, it was practically impossible for them to keep their close formations in good order. All the main tactical formations had been created for an ideal battlefield, consisting of a large plain where the opposing infantry could move without encountering obstacles. In this kind of military system, soldiers were not required to think or act in an autonomous way: they only had to move like clockwork in order to put in practice the orders received. There was no space for initiative, and each infraction of discipline was immediately punished with very harsh methods. In the Prussian infantry, for example, the evolutions required on the battlefield were repeated every day during intensive training sessions that were conducted under the incessant beat of the drums.

During the War of the Austrian Succession, however, some combat actions showed that the Prussian line infantry was not as perfect as it may seem. It became apparent that it could experience serious problems while operating on broken terrain and when fighting against enemy units that employed hit-and-run guerrilla tactics. In particular, the Prussians struggled badly to counteract the efficient light troops deployed by the Austrian Empire, consisting of semi-regular light infantrymen recruited from the inhabitants of the Balkans. The light infantry of the Austrian army had been fighting for decades against the Ottoman Turks on the southern frontier of the Habsburg Empire. They had lived in a state of endless conflict, during which both sides often launched rapid incursions into the territory of the enemy to raid and pillage as much as possible. Gradually, the Austrian frontier soldiers had learned how to fight like their enemies, thereby becoming expert in the art of skirmishing and scouting. Their usual area of operations was covered by mountains and woods, where each soldier had to move singly and not in column or line formation. Most of these soldiers were excellent huntsmen in their civilian life and were also farmers, living on the Balkan frontier as military settlers. As a consequence, their innovative tactics derived from hunting and were based on the tactical principle of open formation, whereby each soldier was to advance in an autonomous way, but keeping contact with the other members of his unit, covering his advance behind obstacles of the terrain (a tree, for example) and firing upon the enemy from a favourable position. The Austrian light infantrymen caused serious troubles and losses for Frederick the Great's perfect line infantry on several occasions. Initially, they were considered as mere murderers by the most traditionalist of their enemies, but during the course of the First Silesian War and Second Silesian War it became apparent that they could play a very important role on the battlefield. The other great powers of Europe, differently from Austria, had no militarized border from which expert light fighters could be recruited, so they started to create their own light infantry formations from the best hunters and gamekeepers of their rural communities. Due to this factor, the new units soon assumed the denomination of Chasseurs or Jagers: both these terms, one in French and the other in German, mean 'huntsmen'. The members of these corps were usually dressed in green, like most of the contemporary civilian hunters, and also like the latter, they communicated with horns and not with drums like the line infantry. From 1740, dozens of new light formations were raised in France and Prussia, following the Austrian example. These proved their efficiency on campaign, confirming that a new branch of the foot troops had been born: the light infantry.

Frederick the Great experienced serious difficulties in forming new light infantry units, mostly because individual initiative and the ability to act out of formation were not compatible with the Prussian Army's disciplinary and tactical systems. The Prussian monarch, like most of his senior officers, had a very negative opinion of light infantry tactics, which he considered as an irritant and ineffective. According to Frederick's tactical view, the Austrian light troops did not pose a real threat to his forces since they had an irregular nature and suffered from a chronic lack of discipline. Being lightly armed, they could only skirmish from distance with the Prussian grenadiers and musketeers, representing a real menace only when they could ambush slow-moving convoys transporting supplies or attack isolated outposts. Frederick was convinced that a simple cavalry screen would be sufficient to prevent the attacks conducted by Austrian light skirmishers against the flanks of his line infantry. Over time, however, he was forced to admit that the Habsburg light troops were not a mere rabble of irregulars and that he had no real means of engaging them on their own light infantry terms. Moral considerations were a serious impediment to the development of light infantry doctrines inside the Prussian Army, since most of Frederick the Great's officers considered sniping or the singling-out of individual targets as a dishonourable military practice. A lightly equipped skirmisher was not perceived as a specialist, but as a coward who killed enemy officers by firing from distance.

As we will see in one of the following chapters, during his long reign, Frederick had to rely on the recruitment of numerous mercenary corps – mostly made up of foreigners – in order to deploy sizeable numbers of light infantry units. Unlike the Austrian Empire, Prussia did not have a militarized border in the Balkans from which thousands of skirmishers schooled in light infantry tactics since childhood could be recruited. The only natural light infantrymen of Brandenburg-Prussia were the gamekeepers and foresters of the realm, who already possessed some skills of woodcraft and of rifle-shooting. It was from these men, who employed rifled carbines during their civilian life for hunting, that the Prussian Army organized its first Jager Corps. In 1740, soon after the outbreak of the First Silesian War, Frederick the Great created the first Korps Feldjager zu Fuss, or Corps of Foot Jagers. This initially consisted of just sixty men, who were all experienced hunters and foresters. The new unit, a single company, was equipped with rifled carbines that were far more accurate than the ordinary line infantry muskets, but much slower and more difficult to reload. Following the achievement of positive results from the initial sixty light infantrymen, Frederick decided to expand the Corps of Foot Jagers. In 1744,

Officer of the 30th Infantry Regiment.

Musketeer of the 30th Infantry Regiment.

it ceased to be an experimental unit and was expanded to comprise two companies, with 150 men each. The Prussian Foot Jagers, being chosen soldiers, enjoyed a series of privileges compared with the ordinary line infantrymen: after completing their period of service with the army, for example, they were offered employment as gamekeepers in the Prussian royal estates. Neither were the light infantrymen subject to the same rigid discipline that terrorized most of the musketeers and grenadiers. After the War of the Austrian Succession, the Foot Jagers were stationed at Mittenwalde in Brandenburg, where they patrolled the mountain passes located on the frontier of their realm. By 1756, the unit had been reorganized as a single company that mustered two officers, six NCOs and 160 privates. Following the outbreak of the Seven Years' War, the Foot Jagers were expanded with the addition of another forty-six privates. On 5 February 1757, a second company was added to the existing one. By March of the same year, another three officers and 100 privates were added to the Corps of Foot Jagers, which came to comprise a total of 300 men. On 10 October 1760, the Prussian Foot Jagers were completely destroyed by the Russian Cossacks at Charlottenburg, after having been surprised by the enemy on open terrain. In 1761, the Corps of Foot Jagers was re-raised in Berlin and Wittenberg, as a single battalion with an internal establishment of four companies. In 1763, following the end of hostilities, the battalion was reduced to just two companies. In 1773, the Battalion of Foot Jagers was expanded and came to comprise five companies, which were increased to six in 1778. In October 1786, a few weeks after Frederick the Great's death, the Battalion of Foot Jagers was doubled in size and became the Regiment of Foot Jagers, which consisted of two battalions with five companies each.

On 24 November 1740, following the creation of the Korps Feldjager zu Fuss, Frederick also raised the Korps Feldjager zu Pferde, or Corps of Mounted Jagers. This was made up of foresters who acted as mounted light infantrymen in order to perform a series of peculiar duties, such as scouting or transporting written messages. Initially, the new corps, which was attached to the General Staff of the Prussian Army, comprised just two NCOs and twelve troopers. The Mounted Jagers came from respected families, meaning their social status was superior to that of the Foot Jagers. During the First Silesian War, the Corps of Mounted Jagers was gradually expanded to comprise 110 men. Between the First Silesian War and the Second Silesian War, the unit was reduced to an establishment of just three NCOs and sixty troopers. In 1744, it was expanded and reorganized on two squadrons, each of which comprised: one officer, three NCOs and 84 troopers. By the outbreak of the Seven Years' War, the Mounted Jagers had various detachments stationed across Brandenburg-Prussia (tasked with fighting contraband) and comprised the following: three officers, ten NCOs and 144 troopers. During the military emergency of 1757, two temporary provincial corps of Jagers were raised from foresters: one with sixty Foot Jagers and forty Mounted Jagers, the other with eighty Foot Jagers and sixty Mounted Jagers. Both corps were disbanded in July 1762.

Uniforms and Equipment

The long reign of Frederick the Great did not see major changes in the uniforms of the Prussian infantry, which remained more or less the same as that worn by them during the later reign of Frederick William I. There were, however, some gradual modifications that took place at a very slow pace: the tricorn hat of the musketeers, for example, had its front peak gradually flattened until the headdress was halfway to becoming a bicorn by the end of Frederick's reign. Military fashions changed and the Prussian Army was sensible to them, like all the other armies of Europe; the basic dress of the Prussian foot troops, however, remained much the same from 1740–86. As we will see, a wide range of regimental distinctions existed, with the various units wearing peculiar variations of the same standard uniform. These regimental variations were sometimes modified over time, being influenced by the personal tastes of the officers commanding the various regiments as well as by the general economic situation. The standard headgear of the musketeers was the black tricorn, which had a narrow lace on the external edge in white or yellow and a button made of white metal or brass at the right front. The tricorn also had a pompom placed on the right front of the top edge and a cord that encircled the crown of the hat (which ended in rosettes at the side corners). Both the pompom and the cord were in a colour scheme distinctive to each regiment. Quite frequently, there was a black cockade over the white metal or brass button. The headgear of the grenadiers was the mitre, which had a tall front made of brass or white metal; this was pointed at the top and bore embossed decorative devices. These decorations were distinctive for each regiment, but usually included a number of common motifs such as the Prussian eagle and the royal cypher of Frederick the Great. Sometimes, the frontal plate of the mitre could be decorated with coloured enamel. The rear of the grenadier headgear consisted of a deep headband, which generally bore decorative badges in white metal or brass reproducing a flame or a grenade. The decorative badges could also represent trophies of arms or cyphers. The cloth placed on the back of the mitre had vertical lace decoration in white or yellow. The frontal plate, at its top point, was surmounted by a pompom that was tufted to resemble a flaming grenade. The pompom was in the same colour scheme distinctive to each regiment that was used for the pompom and cord of the musketeers' tricorn. The grenadier cap was unwieldy and normally had to be tied on by a cord passing under the queue, or plait of hair. The fusiliers wore a mitre that was very similar to that of the grenadiers, but had a lower cloth rear topped by a white metal or brass dome with a small flaming grenade on the top. The cloth rear of the fusiliers' mitre also had three vertical strips in white metal or brass placed on the sides and rear (in place of the vertical lace decoration that was present on the grenadiers' mitre). The standard hairstyle of the Prussian infantrymen consisted of a very long queue bound with black tape, with the side hair generally rolled or curled (with one roll less at the right for musketeers, in order to allow their tricorn to be angled slightly toward the right). Moustaches were compulsory for grenadiers, which they were ordered to tie up at night and to treat with black wax in order to keep them rigid and smooth.

Under the coat, which was the main garment of a Prussian infantryman, a coarse linen shirt was worn. This had a finer linen shirt-front and a stiff linen black stock, which was red rather than black for some regiments. Over the shirt, each soldier wore a single-breasted and collarless waistcoat, which did not have sleeves, was cut longer than waist level and had flapped pockets below the waist at each side of the front. The waistcoat was white for most of the regiments, but some units had it in straw yellow, lemon yellow, rose pink and dark orange. Straw yellow was worn by eighteen regiments, and thus was quite common to see, but rose pink was worn only by the 40th Regiment and dark orange solely by the 49th Regiment. The breeches worn by each infantryman, made of coarse wool with a flap frontal opening, were dyed in the same colour as the waistcoat. The gaiters, extending above the knee and being worn on all occasions, were designed for strength and ease of marching rather than for elegance (according to Frederick's own indication). They were closed down the outer seam by a row of buttons, with a garter placed below the knee. The gaiters were made of linen for parade use and of ticking for campaign use; during the first phase of Frederick's reign, they were white, but over time they became black, which was more serviceable than white and presented a more pleasing appearance. Black gaiters were officially issued for winter dress in 1744, and by the end of the Seven Years' War, the use of white gaiters had also been discontinued for summer dress. Until 1740, during colder months, the Prussian foot soldiers could wear cloaks in order to have some additional protection against bad weather. Soon after becoming king, however, Frederick abolished the use of cloaks in order to cut costs. As a result of this, most of the Prussian soldiers also wore their standard dress when temperatures were extremely low. Only sentries could wear a watch coat, which was not part of their personal clothing but passed from one sentry to his relief. When a Prussian soldier returned to his regiment from furlough, he was instructed to bring with him – at his own expense – a tanned calf-skin and three ells (a unit of measurement roughly

Officer of the 31st Infantry Regiment.

equal to a metre) of coarse linen. These were deposited in the stores of his company and issued whenever he required leather or cloth to repair his shoes or dress.

The standard coat worn by the Prussian infantrymen, though based on the contemporary prevailing civilian style, was not as voluminous as that worn by the foot soldiers of other nations. It was deliberately cut short and close in order to economize on cloth, having tails that extended only so far as the end of the middle finger when the arm was held at the side of the body. The coats had to be worn for two years before being replaced, but they were not produced with materials of good quality. Most of the infantry regiments had coats with frontal lapels, which were originally designed to button across the chest in bad weather, but some regiments had them without lapels as an economy measure. When used, the lapels were usually dyed in the distinctive colour of each regiment. During the later part of Frederick the Great's reign, the lapels of the infantry coats were cut so meanly that they could no longer be fastened over, as had happened previously. The colour of the foot soldiers' coats was the universal and famous Prussian blue, which was relatively cheap to produce but quite elegant. Most of the regiments had coats with folded collars, but some units wore collarless coats. The cuffs could be of two different designs: those of the Prussian pattern were round and had a flap that was generally visible only above the cuff (the flap, however, sometimes extended to the bottom edge of the sleeve), while those of the Swedish pattern – worn by just a limited number of regiments – were gauntlet-shaped with two buttons on the upper edge. The skirts of the coat were turned back in order to reveal the colour of the lining, which was a dull poppy red in most cases. A single shoulder strap, in Prussian blue, was worn on the rear of the left shoulder by all privates (it was not worn by officers and NCOs). The pockets placed at the sides of the skirts were three-pointed and horizontal; they had white metal or brass buttons and were lined red. The vent of each skirt was also lined red and had white metal or brass buttons. The buttons of the coat's breast were generally distributed in pairs, with six on each lapel for lapelled coats or six on the place where lapels would have been for coats without them. An additional couple of buttons were placed at the lower right breast, with corresponding button-holes on the left, sometimes decorated with lace loops. Lace loops were also occasionally present at the rear waist, having only a decorative function. As an important regimental distinction, many of the Prussian infantry regiments had the button-holes placed on the breast of their coat tasselled with decorative loops. These were distinctively Prussian and apparently derived from the cassock, or kaftan, that was extremely popular at the time in Eastern Europe. They could be of various colours and have different shapes; this pattern of decorative lace soon became known as brandenbourg due to its geographical origin.

Fusilier (left) and officer (right) of the 35th Infantry Regiment.

The guard infantry was dressed like the ordinary musketeer regiments, but with more ornate uniforms. The Grenadier-Garde Battalion was uniformed as follows: mitre cap with brass frontal plate, red cloth on the back with golden decorative lace and flaming grenade badges, and red-over-white pompom; Prussian blue coat without lapels, having golden buttons and brandenbourgs, red folded collar and Prussian cuffs, Prussian blue cuff flaps piped in red with four golden brandenbourgs, dark blue shoulder strap piped in red and red turnbacks; buff waistcoat and breeches. The elite 15th Infantry Regiment had two different uniforms: a more ornate parade version that was used by the Leib-Garde or 1st Battalion and a simpler one that was worn by the 2nd Battalion and 3rd Battalion. The Leib-Garde was dressed as follows: black tricorn with black cockade having silver lace holder, large silver edging with decorative embroidering, black and white cord and rosettes; Prussian blue coat without lapels, with silver buttons and brandenbourgs (the latter were tasselled), red folded collar piped in silver, red Swedish cuffs with silver brandenbourgs, silver decorative cords appointed to a shoulder knot of the same colour on the right shoulder and red turnbacks; yellow waistcoat and breeches. The 2nd Battalion and 3rd Battalion of the 15th Infantry Regiment were uniformed as follows: black tricorn with black cockade, silver edging, black and white cord and rosettes; Prussian blue coat with red frontal lapels having silver buttons and white brandenbourgs, red folded collar and Swedish cuffs with white brandenbourgs, silver decorative cords appointed to a shoulder knot of the same colour on the right shoulder and red turnbacks; yellow waistcoat and breeches. The Saxon infantry regiments temporarily absorbed into the Prussian Army continued to be dressed in their usual uniforms, which included black tricorn and a white coat without lapels having facings in regimental colour. Other clothing was also in regimental colour. The garrison infantry regiments and standing grenadier battalions were uniformed with coats that did not have folded collar, frontal lapels and lace. The cuffs were of the Prussian pattern and the tricorn was unlaced. Waistcoat and breeches were Prussian blue (white after 1763). The original four territorial infantry regiments and the militia wore grey coats with blue facings and other items of clothing.

NCOs were uniformed and equipped quite similarly to their men. Sergeants and sergeant majors had silver or golden edging to their tricorn, which had a pompom and corner rosettes in black and white. The coats of sergeants and sergeant majors had silver or golden lace, frequently of a different pattern from that worn by privates. Most of the sergeants and sergeant majors were not equipped with muskets and thus did not have the usual shoulder strap on their coat or a cartridge bow. Other marks of rank employed by NCOs were short gauntlets and a sword knot of mixed black and white (the colours of the Hohenzollerns). Most of the sergeants and sergeant majors carried a cane suspended from a button on the breast, which was used for beating recalcitrant soldiers. Sergeants and 'free corporals' had a 10ft-long half-pike (*Kurzgewehr*) as their main weapon, which was of very limited combat use but worked as a symbol of rank as well as a tool for pushing men into line or for slaying deserters.

Fusilier of the 37th Infantry Regiment.

The uniforms worn by officers were greatly superior to those of the other ranks in terms of manufacture and materials. The officers' tricorn hat had silver or golden edging, which was often scalloped or embroidered to be more ornate. Feathered edging to the tricorn was the distinction of general officers, but was also worn by the officers of the Leib-Garde with their parade dress. The grenadier and fusilier officers wore the tricorn too, instead of the mitre cap used by their men. The officers' coat was a more generous garment than that of the other ranks, having velvet facings and voluminous skirts that in most cases were not turned back. The arrangement of buttons usually followed that of the other ranks, but with more elaborate lace loops on the button-holes. The lace loops embroidered on the officers' uniforms were tasselled brandenbourgs or curving loops of foliate embroidery in the rococo decorative style beloved by Frederick the Great, and were on the breast, cuffs, pockets and rear waist of the coat. The lining of the coat, in most cases, was red, being visible at the edge of the pocket flaps and side-vents. No differentiations of rank existed among the commissioned officers: as a result, the uniform of a general – except for the feathered edging of its tricorn – was identical to that of a captain. The officers' waistcoat and breeches usually matched the colour worn by those of the other ranks, but dark-coloured or black breeches were quite common to find since they were one of Frederick's favoured garments. Officers wore gaiters for dismounted duty and black leather riding boots when mounted; generals, field officers and adjutants usually had horses. Around the waist, under the coat, each officer wore the universal symbol of commissioned rank in the Prussian Army: a silver waist-sash with black interwoven lines, which was knotted at the front of the left hip and had two pendant tassels. While on duty, all officers wore a gorget under their neck that was made of silver and gilt. This could be enamelled and often bore a decorative trophy of arms on the front. The main weapon of officers was a straight-bladed sword with single knucklebow, which was carried on a waist-belt that was largely concealed by the waist-sash. The sword knot was black and silver. Officers, similarly to sergeants and sergeant majors, also carried 8ft half-pikes. The uniforms of the infantry musicians were very similar to those of ordinary privates, but often had elaborate lace decoration on their coat, the design of which was at the discretion of the colonel-in-chief of each regiment. Both narrow and wide laces were used, which could incorporate different symbols and colours. Wide lace was a broader version of narrow lace, being the equivalent of two strips of narrow lace. Most of the musicians had the decorative lace applied around and as vertical stripes upon 'swallow's nest' shoulder wings. In several regiments, the decorative lace also edged the facings and a rosette of lace could be embroidered behind the upper button of the side-vent. Musicians could have decorative lace on the sleeves of their coats, edging the seams and in the shape of chevrons or horizontal bands. Decorative lace might edge the drum-carriage of drummers or the sling for the fife-case of fifers. Drummers wore a leather apron under their coat to protect the leg from wear in the position where their instrument rested. Drums were made of brass and bore an embossed oval trophy of arms with royal cypher on the front. The hoops were coloured according to the personal taste of the colonel-in-chief. The pioneers of each regiment wore a brown leather protective apron and were equipped with a massive axe.

The standard equipment of a Prussian infantryman comprise various very practical elements. At the rear of the right hip, suspended from a whitened buff leather belt up to 5in wide, was a leather cartridge box. This, from 1741 onwards, had provision for sixty rounds. The interior of the cartridge box was compartmented and could be contained in a black leather bag that was usually tied at the top to keep out the rain. The cartridge box was blackened and wax-polished to give a glossy sheen, and was decorated with white metal or brass badges applied on the external surface of its flap. Over the right shoulder, on a narrow white leather belt, a calfskin knapsack was worn by each foot soldier, containing the personal equipment and spare clothing of each infantryman. In 1757, Frederick the Great issued precise regulations detailing the content of the infantry knapsack, which was to consist of the following objects: comb, brush,

Officer of the 38th Infantry Regiment.

looking glass, wax for shoes and moustaches, wooden polishers, a piece of butt leather, screwdriver, spare buttons for the gaiters and a hook for fastening the gaiters. Three tent pegs were usually affixed to the knapsack. Over the right shoulder, each soldier also carried a linen haversack, hanging below the knapsack. A simple tin canteen was carried on top of the knapsack. A sword belt of whitened buff leather was worn around the waist, over the waistcoat, fastened by a rectangular brass buckle. The standard musket fired by the Prussian infantry was based on a pattern that had been introduced in 1723 during the reign of Frederick William I. It was a smoothbore flintlock weapon having a barrel length of about 36in and a wooden stock with very little 'fall-away' towards the butt. The lower edge of the stock was almost straight, yet with an elevated comb on the upper butt. Before 1740, walnut was used to produce the wooden parts of the Prussian infantry muskets, but this was later replaced by the cheaper maple. The wooden components of a musket were treated with a brown paste and then rubbed with oil and wax to help preserve the wood and gave it a high gloss. After the Seven Years' War, the stocks were stained black. The trigger guard, butt-plate, rammer pipes and other fittings of each musket were brass; the iron components were burnished with oil and emery by the regimental armourer and polished every day by the soldiers using a piece of thick leather that was kept in the cartridge box. Fusiliers, being men of smaller stature compared with the musketeers and grenadiers, carried muskets of a slightly reduced length. Frederick William I sponsored the substitution of the old wooden ramrods with new iron ones, which made reloading operations much simpler. During the 1770s, a new model of double-ended iron ramrod was introduced, which was as wide at the bottom as at the top in order to obviate the necessity of reversing the ramrod once it had been drawn. To compensate for the increased weight of the new ramrod, the barrel of the musket used by musketeers and grenadiers was shortened and became the same length as that of the musket employed by fusiliers. From 1776, a leather lock cover for protection of the flintlock mechanism was introduced, attached to the leather sling of each musket. In the 1780s, an improved conical touch hole was introduced, which enabled powder to be forced into the pan from inside the barrel by the action of ramming down the cartridge. This made separate priming unnecessary. Broadly speaking, the M1723 muskets of the Prussian infantry were not very effective weapons: the shape of their stock, together with the length and weight of their barrel, tended to make them so heavy that the muzzles dropped, which resulted in shots falling short. The M1723 musket had a triangular-section bayonet that, from 1741, was fixed permanently when the infantryman was on duty. In addition to his musket, each Prussian foot soldier had a secondary weapon: an infantry sabre with a slightly curved blade and a cast brass hilt with spirally ribbed grip. The sabre had a single knucklebow, ovoid

Officer of the 49th Infantry Regiment.

Fusilier of the 52nd Infantry Regiment.

pommel, shell guards and a slightly downturned rear quillon. Originally designed by Frederick William I, it had a blade about 31in in length; in 1744, Frederick the Great reduced the length of the blade by 6in. The infantry sabre was carried in a leather scabbard that had a metal chape and frog-hook; the chape and throat of the sabre were covered by leather in order to leave only the finial of the chape and the hook visible. A woollen sword knot was wound around the grip and the knucklebow of the sabre, which had a white strap and a tassel in the distinctive colour of each company.

Private of the Corps of Foot Jagers. It was not uncommon for the foot jagers to replace their standard black gaiters with black boots, as shown in this picture.

Private of the Corps of Foot Jagers.

The Foot Jagers were dressed quite similarly to the line infantry's musketeers, but their dress was medium green like the civilian clothes worn by most of the contemporary hunters and foresters. The uniform consisted of the following elements: black tricorn with yellow edging, dark green cockade, black and white cord and rosettes; medium green coat without frontal lapels having brass buttons and yellow decorative cords with a shoulder knot of the same colour on the right shoulder, red folded collar, Swedish cuffs and turnbacks; medium green waistcoat, buff breeches and black gaiters. The Mounted Jagers were dressed very similarly to the Foot Jagers but in dark green: black tricorn with no edging, dark green cockade, black and white cord and rosettes; dark green coat without frontal lapels having brass buttons and yellow decorative cords appointed to a shoulder knot of the same colour on the right shoulder, red folded collar, Swedish cuffs and turnbacks; dark green waistcoat, buff breeches and black leather boots. Officers of both the Foot Jagers and Mounted Jagers had golden brandenbourgs on the button-holes of their coats. The musicians of Foot Jagers were all horn players. The two provincial corps of Jagers formed during the Seven Years' War were dressed with a simplified version of the uniforms described above: black tricorn with no edging, dark green cockade, black and white cord and rosettes; medium green coat without frontal lapels having brass buttons, red folded collar, Swedish cuffs and turnbacks; medium green waistcoat and breeches, and black gaiters or boots. Both the Foot Jagers and Mounted Jagers were equipped with privately purchased rifled carbines and a straight-bladed short sword; the latter had a brass single-bar hilt and was carried from a white leather waist-belt. The sword knot was green for privates/troopers and mixed silver and black for NCOs. The short sword of the Jagers, known as a *Hirschfanger*, could be adapted for use as a bayonet. Instead of the ordinary cartridge box carried on a shoulder belt, the Jagers had a black leather ammunition pouch on the front of their waist-belt (placed over the sword-belt). The horse-furniture of the Mounted Jagers was similar to that of the Prussian Army's dragoons, being dark green with external edge and crowned 'FR' cypher in the rear corners in red.

Chapter 5

The Cuirassiers

History and Organization

The cuirassiers first appeared in European armies during the second half of the sixteenth century, being created to replace the former fully armoured heavy cavalry of the men-at-arms (whose tactics and military traditions went back to the Middle Ages). The introduction of new and smaller firearms that could also be employed on horseback gradually led to the replacement of the heavy lance as the main cavalry weapon with pistols. The new European heavy cavalrymen who dominated the battlefields of the Thirty Years' War (1618–48) were mostly cuirassiers, non-aristocratic mounted fighters who were armed with pistols (in addition to their sword) and no longer used arm or leg armour. These horsemen soon became known as cuirassiers, since they wore armour that was reduced only to the cuirass (originally consisting of both breastplate and backplate). By 1660, most of the European armies had modified the panoply of their heavy cavalry contingents: helmets – which had been popular until that time – gradually fell out of use, together with the backplate of the cuirass. In addition, the pistols lost much of their importance, and most of the cuirassiers started to be equipped only with a long sword that had a straight blade. Combat in the first half of the eighteenth century showed the various military commanders that the cuirasses of the heavy cavalry had lost most of their previous protective function, since the new flintlock muskets of the infantry could easily pierce any kind of cuirass from a certain distance. As a result, some armies, such as those of the French, transformed their cuirassiers into line cavalry by abolishing the use of breastplates. There were, however, several significant exceptions to this rule: Frederick the Great, for example, never deprived his heavy cavalry of cuirasses, as he believed that they could be of great use during close-quarters cavalry combat. The Prussian monarch always had an excellent opinion of his heavy cavalry, considering them an elite shock force that could decide the outcome of a pitched battle with a single frontal charge.

The cavalry that Frederick inherited from his father was not as splendid as the infantry, since it lacked proper training and combat experience. For instance, the cuirassiers were proficient only at ceremonial drill on foot and Frederick claimed that they could not manage their horses in the proper manner. Most of the Prussian cavalry

Officer of the 1st Cuirassier Regiment.

regiments had officers who were totally ignorant of what was required from them in action. The heavy cavalry, in particular, was not capable of manoeuvring effectively, its members often falling from their horses, even on parade. Frederick strove to improve the general quality of his mounted troops through reforming their training

Officer of the 1st Cuirassier Regiment.

and introducing new tactical ideas. He obtained great results in a remarkably short time, mostly because he started assigning the best recruits obtained through the Canton System to the cavalry regiments. The mounted units of the Prussian Army, especially those of cuirassiers, contained the smallest proportion of desertion-prone impressed peasants and unreliable foreign mercenaries. Indeed, the cavalry had to be particularly reliable because it was responsible for discouraging desertion in the infantry units. Most of the Prussian cuirassiers were drawn from the independent peasantry, many of whom had experience of working with horses from their agricultural background. The combat effectiveness of cuirassiers depended upon their physical presence, which was vital for giving the correct impetus to a charge conducted on large horses. Consequently, cuirassiers remained the largest men in the Prussian Army under Frederick the Great, the minimum height required for them being 5ft 5in to keep the riders in proportion to their massive heavy cavalry mounts. Supply of suitable horses always represented a serious problem for Frederick's cuirassiers, who were mostly mounted on the powerful north German breed. The darkest horses were the best in contemporary estimation, and thus were allocated to the heavy cavalry. The protracted campaigns of the Seven Years' War, however, made it impossible for high standards to be maintained, so horses of lighter breed were assigned to the cuirassiers.

Officer of the 2nd Cuirassier Regiment, the only cuirassier unit of the Prussian Army to have a yellow Kollet coat instead of the usual off-white one.

Rigorous training was one of the key factors behind the rapid improvement of Frederick the Great's heavy cavalry. Unlike what happened for the infantry, the Prussian horsemen were given two years of schooling after having been enrolled, which permitted their instructors – who were chosen personally by Frederick – to transform them into excellent riders and disciplined soldiers. The Prussian cuirassiers eventually became capable of lifting their hats off the ground with a sabre while galloping. Training sessions also took place on a regular basis in peacetime, consisting not only of barrack-square manoeuvres but including large-scale exercises that resembled real military campaigns. During these exercises, which were supervised personally by Frederick, the various branches of the Prussian Army learned how to collaborate among themselves in order to conduct combined operations. On paper, each of the three main arms that made up the cavalry – cuirassiers, dragoons and hussars – was capable of performing the duties of the others. This, however, happened only rarely in practice, since the specializations of the various regiments were quite different. The principal tactical unit of the Prussian cavalry was the squadron, for which two methods of approach to an enemy were possible: either at right angles, with the squadrons deploying themselves progressively from line-of-march into line-of-battle, or by having the squadrons move parallel to the enemy and then wheel right or left as necessary. At the beginning of a battle, the cavalry squadrons were formed three ranks deep, though by 1757 a two-rank line had been adopted to compensate for the chronic shortage of men. The second line was frequently used to extend the first if the enemy made a flanking movement, in which case the third line was to replace the second one that had advanced. To permit these movements, the second line had to be deployed at least 300 yards behind the first. The third line had a very important function, since it could be used as a reserve to support a threatened sector of the front or to stall the pursuit of a prevailing enemy. The success of a frontal charge was based on impetuosity, but such a manoeuvre could be effective only if conducted with the right timing. A heavy cavalry charge was built from the trot and delivered at the gallop, which commenced when they were 200 paces from the enemy. It was essential to maintain cohesion until the very moment of impact, in order to maximize the power of the charge. As the charge was delivered, the cuirassiers were to stand in their stirrups and raise their swords in the air, preparing for a downward cut on their enemies' heads or bodies. Frederick the Great, differently from most of the military commanders of his time, preferred launching massive cavalry charges that involved several regiments instead of charges by individual squadrons upon scattered targets. Once a heavy cavalry charge had been delivered, great importance was placed upon the ability to rally quickly and effectively so that it was possible to launch a new charge or resist a counter-charge mounted by the enemy.

Trooper of the 2nd Cuirassier Regiment.

Trooper of the 4th Cuirassier Regiment.

When Frederick became king in 1740, the Prussian Army comprised twelve regiments of cuirassiers, one of which, the 10th Regiment, had an elite status because it was considered the direct heir of the Prussian Gendarmes heavy cavalry of the early eighteenth century. Raising and maintaining a cuirassier regiment had enormous economic costs, as the massive horses and metal cuirasses of the heavy cavalrymen were of far better quality than the mounts and personal equipment of the other cavalry. As a consequence, Frederick formed just one new regiment of cuirassiers during his long reign. This, the 13th Cuirassier Regiment, had guard status since it

Trooper of the 5th Cuirassier Regiment.

was tasked with acting as the mounted bodyguard of the Prussian monarch. Created in 1740 as a single squadron, it bore the denomination of Garde du Corps and was the heir of the military traditions deriving from the corps of that name which existed at the beginning of the eighteenth century). The Garde du Corps was transformed into a regiment in 1756, after two new squadrons were added to its original establishment. For active service, the new 13th Cuirassier Regiment was always brigaded with the 10th Cuirassier Regiment, since it had just three squadrons instead of the standard five deployed by all the other cuirassier regiments of the Prussian Army. Each of the five squadrons that made up a cuirassier regiment had two companies, and a single company consisted of two platoons. A standard squadron consisted of the following elements: six officers, twelve NCOs, two trumpeters, two drummers, two farriers and 150 troopers. Each cuirassier regiment had a small staff, comprising seven officers and ten NCOs.

Uniforms and Equipment

Like those of the infantry, the uniforms of the Prussian cuirassiers did not see any significant modification during the reign of Frederick the Great, being quite elegant and similar to those worn by the heavy cavalry of contemporary European armies. The standard headgear of the cuirassiers was the black tricorn hat, which had internal iron reinforcing bars. Alternatively, a skull cap made of iron or steel – known as a secrete – could be worn under the hat. The secrete was a helmet specifically designed to be concealed beneath the hat and offered excellent protection to its wearer. It was employed by European heavy cavalrymen until the Napoleonic Wars, when most of the cuirassier regiments replaced their tricorn hats with metal helmets. The tricorn of the Prussian cuirassiers had a cord in regimental colour wrapped around the base of its crown and decorative rosettes in regimental colour in its side corners. On the left front of the headgear was a black cockade made of fabric and secured by a black loop; at the lower end of the cockade was a metal button. From 1762, white feather plumes were added to the headgear of the Prussian cuirassiers in order to distinguish them from the Austrian cuirassiers, who wore a very similar uniform. The white feather plumes had a black tip for NCOs and a black base for officers. The most distinctive element of a cuirassier's personal equipment was the cuirass, which consisted of a front-plate only, secured by leather straps that ran along the front of the waist and crossed over the wearer's back. Originally, the straps were made from buff yellow leather, but they became white after the Seven Years' War. The cuirass was enamelled black for all regiments, apart from the 13th Regiment (the Garde du Corps), which had polished cuirasses. The external edges of each cuirass were painted in regimental

Trooper of the 6th Cuirassier Regiment.

Trooper (left) and officer (right) of the 8th Cuirassier Regiment.

colour. The cuirasses of officers had a gilded border set with gilt studs, and on the breast they bore a gilt escutcheon with a crowned royal cypher. The straps of the officers' cuirasses, including those crossing on the wearer's back, were covered with decorative gilt scales (white metal ones for the 13th Regiment). The cuirasses used by officers were edged with scalloped or ruched velvet in regimental colour. Trumpeters did not wear cuirasses. For ceremonial palace duty, as a mark of its household status, the Garde du Corps replaced its metal cuirass with a sleeveless *supreveste*, or tabard. This was red with silver lace decoration down the front, side seams, on the bottom edge, around the neck-holes and around the arm-holes. The *supreveste* had a large silver-embroidered star of the Order of the Black Eagle on the breast, with an orange centre bearing a black eagle as well as a green wreath placed below the Latin motto '*suum cuique*' ('to each his own'). The Order of the Black Eagle was the most important honorific order of Prussia. For officers, the lacing of the *supreveste* was especially fine, the whole garment having a silver fringe around its bottom edge.

The Prussian cuirassiers' uniform was similar to that worn by the heavy cavalry of many European armies, having developed from the leather buff coat – worn under the cuirass – that had been in almost universal use for cuirassier cavalry since the beginning of the seventeenth century. This protective garment, which was not a proper uniform, was also used by the famous Ironsides of Cromwell's New Model Army. During the first years of Frederick's reign, the coat worn by his cuirassiers was straw yellow, a shade that varied from a marked yellow colour to buff or off-white. As it was difficult to achieve a uniform hue due to the variations in the dye, straw yellow was progressively replaced with white. The cuirassier coat, known as a Kollet, had short skirts with wide turnbacks and deep gauntlet-shaped cuffs in the distinctive colour of each regiment. The folded collar was also in regimental colour. The coat did not have lapels or buttons on the chest, being fastened at the waist with hooks and eyes, and its collar did not extend to the front of the neck. A wide strip of lace in regimental colour edged both sides of the breast opening – not quite up to the neck – and continued around the edge of the turnbacks. Similar lace edged the top of the cuffs and their rear opening. The coats of troopers had narrow straps at the rear of the shoulder, in the same colour as the body of the coat; the 10th Regiment had these straps in red, while the 13th Regiment had them in red with a silver centre. The shoulder straps were fastened with a button near the collar, in order to secure the straps of the cuirass. A long-skirted waistcoat was worn under the Kollet; this was in regimental colour, except for the 10th Regiment that had it in dark blue. The waistcoat had edging down the front and around the skirts of narrow lace in regimental colour. The breeches and gauntlets used by cuirassiers were white or off-white, and long white stockings/gaiters were worn under the high-topped black leather riding boots that were peculiar to heavy cavalry. These had spurs attached by strips of black leather. Troopers, differently from officers and musicians, wore a wide girdle in regimental colour around the waist (under the cuirass). The stock was of stiff leather fabric. NCOs wore the same basic uniform as their men, but with some rank distinctions. These included black and white rosettes on the tricorn, a black and white tassel on the sword knot and metallic lace edging to the cuffs of the Kollet.

Trooper of the 10th Cuirassier Regiment (Gendarmes).

Officers' uniforms were made in finer materials and had velvet facings, with all lace – including the loop of the tricorn's cockade – in gold or silver. The hat rosettes of officers were silver with a black centre. Instead of the girdle, officers wore the silver waist-sash with interwoven black lines and fringed hanging ends, which was distinctive of their rank. The officers' sword knots were silver and black. Troopers and NCOs used a small bag made of cloth, known as a sabretache, which was mostly used to carry documents. This piece of equipment was not worn by musicians and officers.

Uniforms worn by the Garde du Corps at the end of Frederick the Great's reign. From left to right: officers with red Galarock coat, officer with parade *supreveste* (tabard) and trooper with parade *supreveste*.

The sabretache had a curved lower edge and the front in regimental colour, while on the front it bore and embroidered royal cypher below a crown. On all but the upper edge, the bag had decorative lace in regimental colour. In addition to the Kollet, the cuirassier officers also possessed a long-skirted frock coat known as a Galarock, which was used for formal occasions. This could be worn over the cuirass, but was more usually worn over a long, straw-coloured waistcoat. The Galarock was white, with gauntlet-shaped cuffs, frontal lapels and folded collar in regimental colour. It had

Officer of the Garde du Corps. The 13th Cuirassier Regiment was the only one to have a polished cuirass instead of the usual one painted in black.

Standard-bearer of the Garde du Corps.

Trooper of the Garde du Corps.

metallic decorative loops embroidered on the button-holes (brandenbourgs): three pairs on each lapel, two loops on each cuff and below each lapel, two loops on each pocket flap and two loops on the rear skirt at waist level. On the right shoulder of the Galarock, a metallic decorative cord (*aiguillette*) was worn. The officers of the 10th Regiment and 13th Regiment had their Galarock in red with blue facings, without lapels. With the parade Galarock, a special version of the tricorn was used with an external edging of scalloped metallic lace. Trumpeters wore a Kollet ornamented with the regimental pattern of musicians' lace: a wide lace on the breast, turnbacks and cuffs, and a narrow lace on the collar, front and rear sleeve seams (in seven horizontal bars on each sleeve). The narrower lace continued as vertical bars upon the 'swallow's nest' shoulder wings that were distinctive of Prussian military musicians. At the rear of the Kollet were two cloth loops hanging from the shoulder, in the same colour as the coat and edged with the musicians' narrow lace (this being a relic of the hanging sleeves worn by heavy cavalry trumpeters during the seventeenth century). The waistcoat of musicians was like that of the ordinary rankers, with standard lace; musicians did not have a girdle, and their waist-belt – worn atop the Kollet – was in whitened buff leather with musicians' lace edging. Both the tricorns and the sword knots of the musicians were like those used by NCOs, except for the hat having a feather edge in regimental colour.

The main weapon of the Prussian cuirassiers was the M1732 Pallasch sword, which had a broad, straight, double-edged blade and a brass semi-basket hilt with large spherical pommel and ribbed leather-covered grip. The solid part of the basket bore an embossed Prussian eagle holding a sceptre, below a large crown, with the royal cypher placed upon the eagle's breast. The sword had a wooden scabbard covered with dark brown or blackened leather, originally having brass mounts, which were changed to iron during the course of the Seven Years' War. The sword knot had a red-brown leather strap and white fringe, the upper sections of the tassel being coloured in white and the distinctive colour of each company. The Pallasch sword was suspended from a waist-belt of red-brown leather, worn beneath the girdle, from a frog or slings. Suspended from the same belt was the sabretache bag. Over the right shoulder (left for NCOs) and atop the cuirass, each heavy cavalryman wore a whitened buff-leather belt holding a black leather cartridge box. The 10th Regiment and 13th Regiment had the belt edged in regimental colour and the cartridge box in white leather. The cartridge box bore an oval brass plate (in white metal for the 13th Regiment) that reproduced the regimental insignia. Over the left shoulder, on top of the cartridge box belt, was a very wide buff leather belt edged in regimental colour; this, which later became whitened, had an iron spring clip to support the carbine worn by each cuirassier at the right side. The carbine and its belt were not carried by officers, NCOs and musicians. A flintlock weapon obtained from the standard infantry musket, the carbine was rarely used by the heavy cavalrymen. Nevertheless, it was carried on the right side of the saddle, with the muzzle in a bucket attached to the lower front of the saddle and the butt held by a leather strap at the upper right. Horse-furniture included a shabraque in regimental colour with rounded rear corners, edged with decorative lace and bearing the regimental device in the rear corners. The shabraque had a matching holster cap on each side of the saddle pommel, since all cuirassiers – including officers, NCOs and musicians – were armed with two flintlock pistols that were employed much more frequently than the carbine. At the rear of the saddle was a valise, atop which was a folded grey greatcoat designed for winter use. In 1756, the expensive greatcoat was replaced with a simpler dark blue cloak. Two designs of shabraque existed for officers: a model for ordinary wear, like that used by troopers except for having metallic lace edging and fringe, and one for parade wear that was rectangular and had double metallic lace edging and fringe (including a Prussian eagle device in the rear corners).

Chapter 6

The Dragoons

History and Organization

The first units of dragoons appeared in European armies during the last phase of the Thirty Years' War, the bloody conflict that ravaged most of Germany from 1618–48. The basic idea behind the formation of the first dragoon corps was to have some soldiers who could move on horseback but fight on foot. The armies of the time increasingly needed highly mobile troops that could travel long distances in a short time but could also fight as standard infantry when needed. As a result, the first companies of dragoons were established, consisting of ordinary infantrymen who knew how to ride a horse and could perform as mounted infantry. The term 'dragoons' derived from the multi-tasking nature of these new soldiers: like the mythical beasts giving them their name, capable of living on earth as well as on water, the dragoons could be employed as infantry but also as cavalry. One of the first armies to include this new type of soldier in large numbers was the French one of Louis XIV, which already had two independent regiments of dragoons by 1660. Initially, these new corps had much more in common with the infantry than the cavalry: they did not wear boots like the ordinary mounted troops, they were organized in companies and not in squadrons, their musicians were drummers and not trumpeters, and their main weapon was an infantry musket and not a cavalry sword. As the eighteenth century progressed, the dragoons partly changed their nature as they started to be employed as mounted infantry only very rarely. On most occasions they were asked to act as proper cavalry, being tasked with conducting frontal charges and other tactical functions that were typical of mounted shock troops. The dragoons gradually became medium cavalry, with equipment that was lighter than the heavy cavalry cuirassiers but heavier than the light horsemen. As a result, a dragoon unit could attack the enemy with a frontal charge but also conduct skirmishing operations in open order. Only in France did the dragoons retain some of their original mounted infantry functions, differently from what happened in the other countries of Europe such as Prussia.

After becoming king, Frederick put great efforts into improving the general quality of his dragoon units, reforming their training and introducing new tactical ideas. He

Troopers (left) and officer (right) of the 3rd Dragoon Regiment, with their pre-1741 white uniform in horse grenadier style (note the use of the mitre cap).

obtained great results in a remarkably short time, largely because he started assigning the best recruits obtained through the Canton System to the mounted regiments. Most of the Prussian dragoons were agricultural peasants with experience of working with horses. Supply of suitable horses was always a serious problem for Frederick's

Trooper of the 6th Dragoon Regiment wearing the white uniform used until 1745.

dragoons, who rode the large and strong north German breed. The protracted campaigns of the Seven Years' War made it impossible for high standards to be maintained, so smaller and lighter horses were assigned to the dragoons. Rigorous training was a key factor behind the rapid improvement of the Prussian cavalry under Frederick, who provided them with two years of schooling after becoming a mounted trooper, allowing their instructors to make them into skilful riders and well-disciplined soldiers. By 1740, the dragoons had completely lost their original mounted infantry character, and despite being considered medium cavalry because they did not wear cuirasses, they were mostly employed to perform the same tactical duties of the cuirassier regiments. Consequently, the tactics and manoeuvres described for the heavy cavalry in the previous chapter were exactly the same as those performed by the dragoon formations. The success of a frontal charge conducted by dragoons was based on their uninhibited nature, but they could only be effective if they were undertaken with perfect timing. It was vital to maintain cohesion until the moment of impact, to maximize the power and effect of the charge. Once a charge had been delivered, it was essential to be able to rally quickly and effectively to allow a further charge or to meet a counter-charge by enemy cavalry.

Trooper of the 1st Dragoon Regiment.

When Frederick became king in 1740, the Prussian Army comprised seven regiments of dragoons; one of these, the 3rd Regiment, had elite status, being styled Horse Grenadiers and wearing a peculiar uniform including a mitre cap. In 1741, however, the Grenadiere zu Pferde (Horse Grenadiers) lost their special status after poor conduct in action and the regiment started to have the same features as a standard dragoon regiment. Raising and maintaining a dragoon regiment had significant economic costs, with the massive horses of the medium cavalrymen being of far better quality than the mounts of the light cavalry. For this reason, Frederick the Great formed

Officer of the 2nd Dragoon Regiment.

just five new regiments of dragoons throughout his long reign. The new units, created between 1740 and 1744, were all formed by detaching squadrons from the existing dragoon regiments; the only exception to this rule was the 12th Dragoon Regiment, which was taken from Wurttemberg service. As we have already seen, it was not uncommon for a major German state like Prussia to purchase the services of an entire military unit from a minor princedom of the Holy Roman Empire. Each dragoon regiment of the Prussian Army mustered five squadrons, except for the 5th Regiment and 6th Regiment, which both had an extra-large establishment with ten squadrons. Each of the five squadrons that made up a standard regiment had two companies, with a single company consisting of two platoons. A standard squadron comprised the following elements: six officers, twelve NCOs, two trumpeters, two drummers, two farriers and 150 troopers. Each dragoon regiment had a small staff consisting of seven officers and ten NCOs.

Drummer of the 2nd Dragoon Regiment.

Uniforms and Equipment

The standard headgear of the dragoons was the black tricorn hat. This had a cord in regimental colour wrapped around the base of its crown and decorative rosettes in regimental colour on its side corners. On the left front of the headgear was a black cockade made of fabric, secured by a black loop; at the lower end of the cockade was a metal button. From 1762, as was the case with cuirassiers, white feather plumes were added to the headgear of the Prussian dragoons to distinguish them from other armies' dragoons. The white feather plumes had a black tip for NCOs and a black base for officers. The headgear of the 3rd Regiment, until 1741, was a mitre cap that had a tall front made of black leather; this was pointed at the top and bore embossed decorative devices in brass. These included the Prussian eagle and the royal cypher of Frederick the Great. The rear of the headgear consisted of a deep headband in black, which bore decorative brass badges reproducing flaming grenades. The black felt placed on the back of the mitre had three vertical strips in brass placed on the sides and rear, and was topped by a brass dome with a small flaming grenade on the top. The grenadier cap was unwieldy and normally had to be tied on by a cord passing under the queue. Under the coat, which was the main garment of a Prussian dragoon, a coarse linen shirt was worn. This had a finer linen shirt-front and a stiff linen black stock. Over the shirt, each soldier wore a single-breasted, collarless and sleeveless waistcoat, which was cut longer than waist level. The waistcoat had flapped pockets below the waist at each side of the front. The colour of the waistcoat was yellow or buff. The breeches and gauntlets used by dragoons could be yellow, buff, white or off-white, while long white stockings/gaiters were worn under the high-topped black leather riding boots. The boots had spurs attached by strips of black leather. The standard coat worn by the Prussian dragoons had all the same general features as that used by the infantry. It was cut short and close to economize on cloth, with tails extending only as far as the end of the middle finger when the arm was held at the side of the body. Most of the dragoon regiments had coats with frontal lapels, which were originally designed to button across the chest in bad weather. Some regiments, however, had coats without lapels in order to cut costs. When used, the lapels were usually dyed in the distinctive colour of each regiment. During the later part of Frederick's reign, the lapels of the dragoon coats were cut so meanly that they could no longer be fastened over, as had happened previously.

The colour of the dragoons' coats was white or off-white for most of the regiments when Frederick was crowned in 1740, but over time this changed because the dragoons of the Austrian army were also mostly dressed in white. By 1745 light blue had become the standard colour for the Prussian dragoons' coats. The 12th Regiment, which had previously been part of the Wurttemberg Army, was dressed

Trooper of the 5th Dragoon Regiment.

Officer of the 6th Dragoon Regiment.

Trooper of the 6th Dragoon Regiment.

in light blue when it was absorbed into the ranks of the Prussians, and it is probable that the new colour was adopted by all dragoon units following the example of the 12th Regiment. Most of the regiments had coats with folded collars, but some units wore collarless coats. The cuffs, like those of the infantry, could be of two different designs: Prussian-pattern cuffs were round and had a flap that was generally visible only above the cuff (the flap, however, sometimes extended to the bottom edge of the sleeve), while those following the Swedish pattern were gauntlet-shaped, with two buttons on the upper edge. Prior to 1745, most of the dragoon regiments had Prussian cuffs, but with the adoption of the new light blue coats, Swedish-style cuffs became

Officer of the 7th Dragoon Regiment.

Officer of the 8th Dragoon Regiment.

predominant. The skirts of the coat were turned back in order to reveal the colour of the lining, which was in regimental colour. The pockets placed at the sides of the skirts were three-pointed and horizontal; they had white metal buttons and were lined in regimental colour. The vent of each skirt was also lined in regimental colour and had white metal buttons. The buttons on the coat's breast were generally distributed in pairs, with six on each lapel for lapelled coats or six where lapels would have been for coats without them. An additional couple of buttons were placed on the lower right breast, with corresponding button-holes on the left; the latter were sometimes decorated with lace loops. Lace loops were sometimes also present at the rear waist, having a decorative function. As an important regimental distinction, many of the Prussian dragoon regiments had the button-holes on the breast of their coat tasselled with decorative loops. These, the famous brandenbourgs, could be of different colours and have various shapes. A single shoulder strap, in the same colour as the coat, was worn on the rear of the left shoulder by all troopers (it was not worn by officers and NCOs). All ranks wore a decorative *aiguillette*, generally yellow, on the right shoulder.

Troopers of the 9th Dragoon Regiment.

NCOs wore the same basic uniform as their men, but with some rank distinctions. These included black and white rosettes on the tricorn, black and white tassel on the sword-knot and a white metal lace edging upon the cuffs. The lace edging was worn by rankers only in the 9th Dragoon Regiment. Officers' uniforms were in finer materials and had velvet facings, with all lace – including the loop of the

Trooper of the 11th Dragoon Regiment.

tricorn's cockade – in golden or silver. The hat rosettes were silver with a black centre. All officers wore the silver waist-sash with interwoven black lines and fringed hanging ends, which was distinctive of their rank. The officers' sword knots were silver and black. The coats worn by officers had metallic decorative loops embroidered on the button-holes (brandenbourgs): three pairs on each lapel, two loops on each cuff and below each lapel, two loops on each pocket flap and two loops on the rear skirt at waist level. On parade, a special version of the tricorn, with the external edging of scalloped metallic lace, was worn. During the period 1740–45, it was not uncommon to see some dragoon officers wearing a cuirass underneath their coats. Dragoon musicians wore distinctive decorative lace to edge the collar, lapels, cuffs, pockets and turnbacks of their coats. The decorative lace, in regimental design, was also embroidered on the rear and side vents of the skirts, the upper button of the side vents being set upon a rosette of lace. On the sleeves, lace was restricted to the bottom edge and vertical bars of the 'swallow's nest' shoulder wings. The tricorn of musicians was like that of rankers, with no feathered edging. Dragoon drummers carried brass infantry-style side drums, carried on a wide leather belt worn over the right shoulder that was edged with regimental lace (which also ran across the loops that held the drumsticks).

The Prussian dragoons' main weapon was the M1735 Pallasch sword, with its broad, straight, double-edged blade and a brass four-bar semi-basket hilt. Two of the bars intersected with a brass disc where they joined, with a short quillon at the rear and a half-shell on the opposite side of the basket. An eagle-head pommel and a leather grip bound with brass wire completed the structure of the sword. The wooden scabbard was covered with dark brown or blackened leather, originally having brass mounts that were changed to iron during the course of the Seven Years' War. The sword knot had a red-brown leather strap and white fringe, the upper sections of the tassel being coloured in white and the distinctive colour of each company. The Pallasch was suspended from a white leather waist-belt, from a frog or slings. No sabretache bag was carried. Over the left shoulder, each dragoon wore a whitened buff-leather belt with a black leather cartridge box, which featured a white metal plate that reproduced the regimental insignia. The belt also supported the carbine, which was of an intermediate length between the infantry musket and the shorter cuirassier carbine. It was equipped with a bayonet and had its own leather sling. The carbine was not carried by officers, NCOs or musicians. It was carried on the right side of the saddle, with the muzzle in a bucket attached to the lower front of the saddle and the butt held by a leather strap at the upper right. Horse furniture included a shabraque in regimental colour with rounded rear corners, edged with decorative lace and bearing the regimental device in the rear corners. The shabraque had a matching holster cap on each side of the saddle pommel, since all dragoons – including officers, NCOs and musicians – were armed with two flintlock pistols that were employed much more frequently than the carbine. At the rear of the saddle was a valise, on top of which was carried the folded grey greatcoat designed for winter use. In 1756, the greatcoat was replaced with a simpler light blue cloak. Two designs of shabraque existed for officers: one for ordinary wear that was like that used by troopers, except for having metallic lace edging and fringe, and one for parade wear that was rectangular and had double metallic lace edging and fringe (including a Prussian eagle device in the rear corners).

Chapter 7

The Hussars

History and Organization

During the early eighteenth century, heavy cavalry was the most important component of the European mounted troops, making up the bulk of the cavalry forces mobilized by the various nations and having progressively acquired tactical supremacy on the battlefields on the Continent. Well-trained and highly disciplined, the heavy cavalry consisted of horsemen armed with long, straight-bladed swords and mounted on massive horses, able to charge and manoeuvre on the battlefield in perfect order by maintaining knee-to-knee close formations. This kind of cavalry was mostly employed to conduct frontal charges and to cover the retreat of routed line infantry. However, the situation began to change after the Thirty Years' War, when cavalry had started to perform a series of auxiliary roles for the infantry and was rarely used independently. There were, however, some exceptions to this general rule: in Eastern Europe, some alternative kinds of cavalry – having lighter equipment and peculiar tactical duties – had started to develop from the second half of the sixteenth century. Since 1550, Poland had been the homeland of a new kind of cavalry armed with lances, whose members were known as uhlans and soon became the national cavalry of the Polish state. The uhlans were extremely versatile and tactically flexible: being lightly equipped, they could easily act as explorers or skirmishers; and being armed with lances, they could also charge against enemy infantry or fight large-scale cavalry battles. The Polish lancers became increasingly famous for their mastery in the use of the lance, which gave them a great advantage over enemy horsemen who were armed only with much shorter swords or sabres. A Polish uhlan could kill his cavalry opponents from distance by using a weapon that was very simple and cheap to produce compared with a sword or sabre. Meanwhile, in Hungary, light horsemen known as hussars gradually came to dominate the local battlefields from 1550 onwards. The etymology of the word 'hussar' is not very clear, with several theories having been elaborated in order to explain how this term came to indicate the light cavalrymen of Hungary. Most etymologists and historians, however, agree on the fact that the word could come from the Hungarian '*huszár*', a modified version of the medieval Serbian '*husar*', a word that was used to indicate the

Officer of the 1st Hussar Regiment.

Officer of the 2nd Hussar Regiment.

mounted brigands who harassed the peasant communities living in the countryside of the Balkan nations.

In 1526, the expanding Ottoman Empire of the Turks defeated and invaded the large Kingdom of Hungary, which, together with Poland, had been one of the leading political and military powers of Eastern Europe during the Middle Ages.

Colour plate showing the uniform worn by the 2nd Hussar Regiment during the early part of Frederick the Great's reign. From left to right: officer, drummer, officer and trumpeter.

The Ottomans occupied most Hungarian lands, but not the region of Transylvania, which retained a degree of autonomy. During the second half of the sixteenth century, Hungary became the main battleground for the bloody wars that took place between the Habsburg Empire and the Ottoman Empire. These conflicts, which continued for most of the seventeenth century, were mostly fought for possession of Hungary, with the Habsburgs determined to eradicate the Turkish presence in the northern Balkans – which represented a serious threat to the political stability of their Austrian homeland. Initially, the Ottomans obtained a series of victories during these wars, but over time the Habsburgs gained the upper hand. By the end of the seventeenth century, Transylvania had been annexed to the Austrian Empire, together with some other Hungarian territories, while the Habsburgs had also started to exert their political control over Croatia (which had been a vassal state of Hungary for most of the Middle Ages). During the seventeenth century, the Balkans were almost constantly at war, both the Habsburgs and the Turks employing bands of irregulars to conduct raids across their respective borders, even when there was no 'official' conflict going on. These irregulars, seen as simple brigands by the local communities, acted autonomously and had no military discipline to speak of. They pillaged the frontier territories of their enemies and killed civilians with no mercy, earning a living by seizing land. These early hussars were not paid for their services but were of great use for both the Habsburgs and the Ottomans, who could thus maintain a state of war on the Balkan frontier without deploying their regular troops in that theatre of operations (which had significant economic costs). The harsh nature of the local terrain and the tactical duties that they had to perform made the hussars a very distinctive category of mounted troops. In order to move rapidly across the hills and woodlands of the Balkans to conduct their guerrilla operations, they had to be mounted on agile but sturdy horses and to carry light equipment consisting of offensive weapons only (they wore no helmets or armour, in order to have a higher degree of mobility). The Habsburgs tried to regularize their bands of hussars recruited from Hungary and Croatia, understanding that these mounted skirmishers could be of great use in other theatres of operations outside the Balkans. In the early decades of the seventeenth century, the hussars started to add light firearms to their equipment, and a good number of them – mostly coming from Croatia – were employed in Central Europe during the Thirty Years' War. Both the Austrians and their opponents were much impressed by the combat skills of the hussars, who were able to conduct highly effective reconnaissance missions as well as to harass enemy columns by using hit-and-run tactics. France, among Austria's main enemies during the Thirty Years' War, was one of the first European nations to recruit irregular contingents of Croatian mercenaries for service within its military forces. During the late seventeenth century, the Habsburgs started to recruit regular units of hussars from their Hungarian lands, the semi-autonomous Principality of Transylvania having finally been annexed by the Habsburgs. The new hussar corps of the Austrian army performed very well during the War of the Spanish Succession, showing great valour as effective skirmishers and explorers. Consequently, in the years

Colour plate showing the uniform worn by the 2nd Hussar Regiment during the late part of Frederick the Great's reign. From left to right: troopers and NCO.

that followed the end of the conflict, most of the major European armies formed their own units of hussars. Prussia was no exception to this rule, their combat experience in both the War of the Austrian Succession and Seven Years' War confirming the tactical importance of these new light cavalry troops. A new form of warfare had been born: the *petite guerre*, or little war, which was based on low-intensity combat and hit-and-run tactics.

Colour plate showing the Polish-style uniform of the short-lived Corps Hulaners of 1741–42, later transformed into the 4th Hussar Regiment.

Trooper of the 4th Hussar Regiment with the first headgear worn by his unit (a black mirliton).

Frederick the Great understood the great potential of the hussars as skirmishers and explorers before becoming king, so after 1740 he endeavoured to enlarge the light cavalry component of his army (which had been quite weak under Frederick William I). The new monarch, as we have seen in the previous chapters, was not a revolutionary innovator regarding heavy and medium cavalry tactics, but he was a great modernizer with light cavalry tactics, being the first major non-Austrian king to employ hussars as a fundamental component of his mounted forces. According to Frederick's tactical views, skirmishing and scouting were the two fundamental elements of what he called hussar service. While reconnoitring, hussars were exhorted not to engage the enemy but to behave with circumspection and to remember that their task was to gather information. When skirmishing, the hussars had to be deployed so that only one troop from each squadron fired from the saddle; the remaining troops were to be kept in close order in readiness to engage the enemy with sabre in hand. When confronting Austrian light troops, Frederick ordered that his hussar skirmishers should always advance hastily and attack the enemy in close order. Indeed, the light contingents in Habsburg service could not endure – in most cases – a direct confrontation with the aggressive Prussian hussars. If attacked by enemy skirmishers, Frederick's hussars were usually ordered to charge against their opponents instead of firing from distance in open order. Furthermore, Frederick instructed that, when withdrawing, his skirmishers should move as slowly as possible and contest every defile or bridge; it was in such cases that the fire of carbines could offer a good screen for protection of the troops that were retreating. Despite the emphasis placed on the use of the sabre, hussars were taught how to fight on foot if needed. Their superior morale and discipline enabled them to face any kind of enemy, even line infantry advancing in close formation.

Whereas Frederick the Great inherited most of his heavy and medium cavalry from his father, the light regiments were largely his own creation. The Prussian Army had included some small hussar contingents since 1721, but by 1740 these had seen very little expansion. When Frederick became king, the Prussian military mustered just nine squadrons of hussars: three of Leib-Husaren, or Regular Hussars, and six of Preussische Husaren, or Prussian Hussars. The latter were the first to be formed, when two companies of hussars were raised in 1721 and attached to the 6th Dragoon Regiment. These were expanded to become three squadrons in 1730 and then six squadrons in 1739. The Leib-Husaren were formed in 1730 as a single company raised from Berlin. In 1733 they were expanded to three squadrons, and in 1736 they received the denomination of Regular Hussars since they were not attached to a dragoon regiment like the Prussian Hussars. During the First Silesian War, the hussars of the Prussian Army fought with great distinction, but Frederick found that there were hopelessly too few of them to match up with the Austrian light troops. Frederick also realized that good hussars did not have to be necessarily Hungarians; as a result, he decided to expand his light mounted troops significantly. The Preussische Husaren were expanded to eight squadrons in 1740 (ten by 1742) and were transformed into the 1st Hussar Regiment. Meanwhile, the Leib-Husaren were expanded to ten squadrons and became the 2nd Hussar Regiment. In 1740, a new 3rd Hussar Regiment was created from the former 1st Squadron of the Prussian Hussars, the unit having ten squadrons by 1742. The 4th Hussar Regiment was formed in 1741 from Polish deserters of the Austrian army, initially consisting

Officer of the 4th Hussar Regiment with the second headgear worn by his unit (a black busby).

Trooper of the 4th Hussar Regiment.

of six lancer squadrons collectively known as the Corps Hulaners, or Uhlan Corps. In 1742, it was transformed into a hussar regiment. The 5th Hussar Regiment – the famous Death's Head Hussars Regiment – and 6th Hussar Regiment were both raised in 1741 by detaching some squadrons from the 1st Regiment and 2nd Regiment, meaning the Prussian Army now mustered six regiments of hussars.

The 7th Hussar Regiment and 8th Hussar Regiment were formed in 1743. During the Seven Years' War, in 1758, the 9th Hussar Regiment was created. During the Battle of Maxen, which took place in November 1759, the 8th Hussar Regiment was annihilated by the Austrians, leaving the Prussian cavalry with only eight regiments of hussars that were renumbered in order to replace the unit that had disappeared. Each hussar regiment consisted of ten squadrons, a single squadron comprising the following elements: three officers (four in the six senior squadrons), eight NCOs, one trumpeter, one blacksmith, one medical assistant and 102 troopers. No regimental staff existed, since the various units were rarely deployed in regimental strength and their individual squadrons mostly acted independently. In 1771, a new hussar regiment was raised, which became the 9th Hussar Regiment, followed by the 10th Hussar Regiment in 1773. The 9th Hussars, despite its official denomination, was a lancer unit that had a peculiar history.

It was made up of Bosniak mercenaries from the militarized frontier that divided the Austrian Empire from the Ottoman Empire in the Balkans. The unit was originally raised for service in the Saxon Army by an Albanian jeweller named Stephan Serkis, who also recruited lancers for the new corps from the Cossacks of Ukraine. Unable to enlist his mercenary soldiers in Saxon service, Serkis offered them to Frederick the Great, who attached the squadron of Bosniaken to his 5th Hussar Regiment in 1745. The Balkan lancers performed very well during the Second Silesian War, being the only mounted unit of the Prussian Army equipped with lances. As a result, after the Seven Years' War broke out, the Bosniaken – who were comparable to the Polish uhlans in terms of combat ability – were progressively expanded with the recruiting of new Balkan mercenaries in order to become a regiment with ten squadrons. With the end of hostilities in 1763, they went back to their original establishment with a single squadron. In 1770, the Bosniaken were expanded to five squadrons, and in 1771 they received the new denomination of the 9th Hussar Regiment despite being a lancer corps. In 1773, their establishment was increased to ten squadrons, but they remained associated with the 5th Hussar Regiment until they were granted their own colonel-in-chief in 1788.

Officer of the 5th Hussar Regiment, the famous unit known as the Death's Head Hussars because of its black uniform and *Totenkopf* symbol (consisting of a skull above two crossed bones).

Uniforms and Equipment

Each regiment of hussars of the Prussian Army had a uniform in a distinctive colour, but the general pattern of the dress was similar for all units since it was based on the traditional costume of the Hungarian light cavalrymen in Habsburg service. The headgear was a fur busby for the first four regiments and a felt mirliton for the remaining ones. The busby, at least during the years of the First Silesian War, was quite low – only about 6in deep – but it gradually increased to 11–12in. The fur used to produce this kind headgear was usually medium brown, being bearskin in most cases, although wolf fur and marten fur were also used. Decorative cords encircled the top of the busby and fell at the right side; these were in white metal or brass for troopers (silver or golden for officers, black and white for NCOs) and ended in tasselled *raquettes* that were in the distinctive colour of each squadron. A bag of cloth in regimental colour fell at the side or rear of the busby. The mirliton cap was made of black felt and was 9–11in high, but increased in size over time, just like the busby. It had a black triangular wing that was wound around its main body or allowed to fall free, which had a white metal or brass coloured tassel at the end (this was black and white for NCOs). Decorative cords encircled the top of the mirliton and fell at the right side; these were in white metal or brass for troopers (silver or golden for officers, black and white for NCOs) and ended in tasselled *raquettes* in the distinctive colour of each squadron. The wing was edged in silver or gold for officers and in black for NCOs, who also had a rosette in the distinctive colour of their squadron on the front of the mirliton. Hussar officers, especially the more traditionalist ones, could sometimes wear a standard black tricorn hat instead of the Hungarian busby or mirliton. From 1762, a white plume was added to the standard headgear of the Prussian hussars, exactly as happened for cuirassiers and dragoons. The Hussars' hair was gathered into a queue, which was much shorter than that worn by cuirassiers and dragoons, while troopers were permitted to wear twists of hair hanging from the temples. Moustaches were worn by all ranks except for musicians.

The hussar jacket, known as the dolman or kamisol, was tailless and had a standing collar. On its front were three rows of buttons, the central one being made up of 'ball' buttons and the outer ones flat buttons. There could occasionally be four outer rows instead of two, but this happened quite rarely. Cord frogging or braid edged the collar and cuffs, which were pointed and could have a decorative loop embroidered at their point. Horizontal lines of braid linked the buttons on the breast, these braid loops sometimes being interlaced at the ends. By the time of the First Silesian War, the breast loops were short but they later spread to the extent of the chest. The number of lines of braid varied from a minimum of ten to a maximum of eighteen. Officers' lace was silver or golden, and the extent of decoration was greater than that of the other ranks. This included 'figuring' around the cuffs, in addition to a broad lace cuff edging. Troopers and NCOs had diamond-shaped or heart-shaped leather patches reinforcing the elbows of their dolman. Over the dolman, all hussars wore the short pelisse jacket, probably the most distinctive garment of the Hungarian-style light cavalry. This was worn slung upon the left shoulder in full dress but was rarely seen on campaign, except during cold months when it was worn as a normal jacket over the dolman. The pelisse was braided in a similar way to the dolman, but was lined and edged with fur. The pelisse was in the same contrasting colour as the dolman's standing collar and pointed cuffs; as a result, each hussar regiment had two

Trooper of the 5th Hussar Regiment.

Trooper of the 5th Hussar Regiment.

Trumpeter of the 5th Hussar Regiment.

distinctive colours – one for the dolman and another for the pelisse and the facings of the dolman. In addition to the usual practice of identifying regiments by the name of their colonel-in-chief, hussar units were also known by the colour of their uniform. All ranks wore light buff-coloured buckskin breeches in summer and similarly coloured cloth breeches in winter, with cloth leggings extending to the upper thigh over the breeches. These garments were edged with lace, as on the dolman. Until the end of the Seven Years' War, they generally had a heart-shaped patch of the dolman colour, edged with regimental braid (sewn above the knee). Strips of braid started to be added to the rear seam of the leggings, which were in the same colour as the dolman.

Boots were of the traditional Hungarian pattern, extending to the bottom of the knee at the front and being lower at the back, with iron heels and iron spurs plugged in. Officers sometimes used longer boots made of yellow leather, especially for full dress. A barrelled sash was worn over the dolman but beneath the pelisse, which in most cases was in the same colour as the dolman's collar and cuffs and had interwoven lines in a contrasting colour. The barrelled sash of officers was silver and black. A waist-belt made of brown leather (covered with silver or golden lace for officers), with five slings, was used to hold both the sabre and the sabretache bag, the latter being the most distinctive element of a hussar's personal equipment. The sabretache was brown or black leather, with a regimentally coloured cloth flap on the front that bore a crowned royal cypher and wide lace edging in white metal or brass. The sabretaches of officers were more ornate and usually featured a white shield bearing a black Prussian eagle, a crown and a trophy of arms (all reproduced in decorative metallic embroidery). Trumpeters' uniforms were like those of the troopers, but had 'swallow's nest' shoulder wings ornamented with regimental musicians' lace (only on the pelisse). All trumpeters wore the mirliton, even in regiments that otherwise had the busby as headgear. The wing of the mirliton used by musicians could be in the same colour as their dolman's collar and cuffs. Musicians' plumes were originally in regimental colouring, but over time they became red or red with a white tip. The cartridge box of the hussars was brown leather or black, with a belt of the same material, and was worn over the right shoulder by troopers and on the left shoulder by officers and NCOs. Both the cartridge box and its belt were laced in silver or gold for officers.

Troopers were armed with a carbine, which was quite similar but a bit shorter than that carried by cuirassiers, although ten hussars in each squadron had a rifled version of this weapon for skirmishing. The carbine was attached to a plain belt in buff or whitened leather, which was worn over the left shoulder. This had brass fittings and an iron carbine clip. The main weapon of the Prussian hussars was a sabre, which had a curved black and iron stirrup-shaped hilt. This was carried in a wooden scabbard covered with black leather that had an iron throat and chape. The sword knot was made of black or brown leather for troopers, but was white and black for NCOs and silver and black for officers. All ranks carried two flintlock pistols in holsters that were placed beneath the front of the shabraque, which had pointed rear corners and no holster caps; it was in the same colour as the dolman, with 'vandyke' edging in the same colour as the dolman's facings for troopers/NCOs and in silver or gold for officers. The full-dress shabraques for officers had a distinctive decoration in the rear corners, consisting of a gold-crowned white shield bearing a black Prussian eagle. At the rear of the saddle, each hussar had a cylindrical valise in the same colour as the shabraque, with circular ends trimmed in the same colour as the dolman's facings. The valise rested upon an unbleached fabric fodder sack, and on top of the valise was the folded cloak for winter use, which had a wide collar. The cloak was white

Officer (left) and trooper (right) of the 6th Hussar Regiment.

Trooper of the 8th Hussar Regiment.

Officer (left) and trooper (right) of the Bosniaken, wearing the first uniform of their unit.

or in the same colour as the dolman. Horse harnesses, in Hungarian style, were black or dark brown leather.

The original uniform of the exotic Bosniaken was in a distinctive semi-oriental style, which was retained even when deserters of various nationalities were recruited to replace the original Balkan members of the unit. As headgear, it included a white turban wrapped around a red skull cap, having a red and white feather on the left. The main garment of the uniform was a red jacket having the same length as a dolman with white lace edging around the collar, cuffs, down the breast edge and on the bottom edge. The pointed cuffs bore a white loop and the breast did not have buttons. Over the jacket, a long-skirted black overcoat with folding collar and wide elbow-length sleeves was worn. This had white lace around the edges and on the bottom of the sleeve. Turkish-style baggy trousers, in red with white lace on the outer seam, completed the outfit. Belt equipment was black leather and the black cartridge box bore a white metal royal cypher on its flap. The shabraque was black with red 'vandykes' and had black holster caps with red 'vandykes'. The holster caps bore a royal cypher embroidered in white. Three tassel-ended laces were on the breast of the jacket and overcoat for both officers and NCOs (being in silver for officers and white for NCOs). The early uniform of the Bosniaken corps described above was changed after the end of the Seven Years' War. The original semi-oriental appearance was retained in the unbraided red jacket and baggy trousers, both laced in

Officer of the Bosniaken, wearing the second uniform of his unit.

Colour plate showing the second uniform of the Bosniaken; the figure on the left is wearing the winter version, with black frock coat.

white as before, but the trousers had vertical side-pockets piped in white and white piping around some red cloth reinforcing that was placed around the ankle. The new headgear was a dark brown fur cap, similar to the busby worn by hussars. It had no hanging bag but a red cloth crown, with white cords and *raquettes* hanging at the right. The white plume introduced for all cavalry regiments from 1762 was also worn by the Bosniaken on their headgear. Rankers wore a red girdle, which was black and white for NCOs; officers had a silver and black sash. Belt equipment continued to be black leather, with the cartridge box belt being worn over the left shoulder by troopers and over the right shoulder by NCOs. Like for the hussars, Bosniaken troopers were armed with a short carbine and wore a white carbine belt over their left shoulder, while attached to the spring clip of the carbine belt there was a flintlock pistol. Officers, with the introduction of the new uniform, were given a peculiar dress, consisting of a red frock coat with three rows of buttons and silver hussar-braid on the breast. The frock coat also had silver piping outlining its vertical side pockets and black facings (folded collar and pointed cuffs) piped in silver. In winter, all ranks wore a very long black frock coat with black cuffs over their usual dress. The falling collar and lining of the frock coat were of off-white or pale grey fur, with white piping and no buttons down the breast. There was white piping too around the bottom edge and on the vertical pockets of the frock coat. NCOs had silver lace on the upper edge of the cuffs – as on the red summer jacket – and three tassel-ended white lace loops on each side of the upper breast. In winter, the girdle was worn over the black frock coat. The latter, for officers, had silver piping to the cuffs as well as around the pockets and down the front/bottom edges. It had a red folding collar piped in silver. Its breast bore three rows of buttons and tassel-ended loops of hussar-style braid in silver. Trumpeters were dressed like troopers, but with black shoulder wings on their original overcoat which had white lace with a red stripe. Their headgear was a red mirliton with black wing, red rosette on the front and a white plume with red base. With the introduction of the new uniform, the trumpeters of the Bosniaken started to be dressed like troopers, but with mixed red and white piping and with distinctive lace on both the collar and cuffs of their jackets. The musicians' black winter frock coat had mixed red and white piping, distinctive lace on the cuffs and three mixed red and white tassel-ended loops on the upper breast. From their formation, the Bosniaken carried lances, usually having the shaft painted in red and black spirals. The lances had a swallow-tailed pennon in the distinctive colour of each company (later of each squadron, when the unit was expanded). The officers and NCOs had lances with black over white pennons; the black part bore a golden sun badge and the white part a gold-crowned black flying eagle. The officers' pennons were made of silk, and the shafts of lances carried by officers were painted white. All ranks, in addition to the lance, carried the same sabre used by the hussars.

Chapter 8

The Artillery and Technical Corps

History and Organization

Frederick the Great was not renowned as a great artillery commander, considering his gunners to be second-rate soldiers compared with his highly disciplined infantrymen. The officers of the Prussian artillery, when Frederick became king, were mostly cliquish and inward-looking, having never received any special attention from Frederick William I. The gunners under their orders had low morale and were seen as a secondary component of the Prussian Army, only being allowed to carry muskets in emergencies. Yet although Frederick did not appreciate the minutiae of artillery techniques, he recognized the importance of field guns during pitched battles, greatly expanding the number of his artillery and significantly improving artillery tactics. In 1740, like that of other armies, the Prussian artillery was divided into position guns and battalion guns. The former were of larger calibre but were quite static, while the latter were lighter pieces, each crewed by four gunners and four infantrymen, which accompanied infantry regiments to provide immediate fire support. By the end of the eighteenth century, it was acknowledged almost universally by military commanders that battalion guns attached to the infantry were not very effective, and that the effect of a concentration of artillery fire exceeded the sum of its parts. Despite this, however, Frederick persisted with battalion guns. Since 1731, the Prussian artillery had been restricted to four calibres, of which the 3-pdr and 6-pdr guns were used for battalion guns for infantry support. The 6-pdr field gun that Frederick the Great inherited from his father's artillery reforms of 1731 required a five-horse team to be transported, and thus was considered insufficiently mobile. Consequently, it was replaced in 1742 by a new 3-pdr field gun that was much lighter. This, drawn by just three horses, had a chambered breech that required a smaller charge. During the same year, Frederick also introduced limbers with ammunition boxes, a technical improvement that increased the mobility of the Prussian field pieces. Nevertheless, the new 3-pdr field gun proved to have less hitting power than the old 6-pdr version, and thus was not particularly effective on the battlefield. As a result, in 1755, two new field guns were designed to replace it: a lighter 6-pdr gun (with a four-horse team) and a longer-barrelled 3-pdr gun. Battalion guns were

Colour plate showing the uniforms of the Prussian artillery. From left to right: bombardier, gunner and officer.

usually allocated at a rate of two per regiment, and Frederick's intention was to use the new lighter 6-pdr gun for first-line units and the long-barrelled 3-pdr gun for second-line units. This, however, was not always possible. From 1758, the two guns assigned to each regiment were supplemented by a new 7-pdr light howitzer, which proved so effective that one was attached to every infantry battalion by the end of the Seven Years' War. By 1758, Frederick was forced to introduce new models of 3-pdr and 6-pdr battalion guns, the previous ones having proved to be no match for the new Austrian artillery during the first phase of the Seven Years' War. The new guns had fully bored breeches instead of the unsuccessful chambered breeches of the previous models.

In 1770, the guns introduced in 1758 were themselves replaced, this time by new long 3-pdrs and light or heavy 6-pdrs. The position guns were heavy 12-pdrs and 24-pdrs, which were intended for battery fire as an artillery reserve and were immensely more effective than the lighter and dispersed battalion guns. The old 12-pdrs and 24-pdrs were replaced with new chambered versions from 1754. The 12-pdr gun was the standard battery cannon of the Prussian artillery, with an eight-horse team. The new chambered bore, as had happened with the battalion guns, proved less effective, so Frederick was compelled from 1757 to employ older and heavier 12-pdrs with twelve-horse teams that were originally intended for garrison use. These were quite effective and remained in service for a long time alongside the new chambered guns. The Prussian position guns also included 12-pdrs of medium weight, with ten-horse teams, patterned on those of the contemporary Austrian artillery. Recognizing the utility of high-angle fire, Frederick the Great improved the heavy 18-pdr howitzer that he inherited from his father and also introduced new 10-pdr and 18-pdr howitzers during 1743 and 1744. A new version of the 10-pdr howitzer came into use after the Seven Years' War. Until 1759, the Prussian artillery also included a heavy 24-pdr positional cannon, which was so ponderous in movement that from 1759 it was withdrawn from field use and assigned to siege/garrison duty. The guns employed for siege/garrison duty mostly consisted of 10-pdr, 24-pdr and 50-pdr mortars. All the guns of the Prussian artillery were brass smoothbores, having carriages painted in light blue.

The Prussian artillery had no permanent train corps, like in most contemporary European armies. The horses, ammunition waggons and drivers needed to move the guns and equipment of the various batteries were all impressed from civilian sources at the beginning of a campaign and discharged upon its conclusion. They were commanded by a small number of officers and NCOs, who were supplemented with craftsmen and – from 1760 – by tiny cavalry detachments tasked with escort duties. Since the artillery drivers were civilians, only the heaviest position guns were dragged by their teams to the battle line, but the battalion guns were unlimbered at a considerable distance from the enemy and hauled into place by artillerymen by means of leather and rope straps. No use was made of other more modern methods of moving field guns. The dispersal of teams and drivers at the end of a campaign resulted in there being virtually no mobile artillery in peacetime: guns were returned to their depots and field exercises were only held for a few weeks annually. This gave few opportunities to the artillery to learn how to cooperate with other branches of service. The tactical employment of field guns varied considerably, according to circumstances. During the War of the Austrian Succession, Frederick the Great

Officer (left), private in working dress (centre) and NCO (right) of the Pioneer Regiment.

employed a mixture of concentration and dispersal of fire, positioning howitzers and 24-pdrs on the flanks of his line and using 12-pdrs as supplements to the lighter battalion guns. Position batteries, however, were also employed as a reserve, which was usually placed upon high ground. Frederick occasionally employed his heavy guns to perform an offensive role, opening an effective barrage on the enemy that accompanied the attacks of the infantry or cavalry. Combat experience from the Seven Years' War showed the Prussian monarch that massed batteries could concentrate their fire upon blowing holes in the enemy line, a tactical concept that was fully developed by Napoléon some decades later. From 1760, Frederick distributed his heavy artillery into ten-gun batteries among his infantry units, a tactical return to the past of the battalion guns, which was mostly determined by the decreasing quality of the Prussian infantry regiments.

When Frederick became king, the artillery of the Prussian Army consisted of one field battalion with six companies – commanded by the expert General Christian von Linger, who had reformed the Prussian artillery in 1731 – and four garrison companies stationed in the fortresses of Pillau, Magdeburg, Stettin and Wesel. In 1741, a second field battalion was raised, having one bombardier and five cannoneer companies like the existing one. The bombardiers were intended to serve howitzers and mortars, while the cannoneers were tasked with serving field guns. A fifth garrison company was raised for service in newly conquered Silesia in 1742 and was posted at Breslau. In 1744, the two field battalions were assembled together to form a single regiment known as the Feldregiment Artillerie. In 1758, the internal establishment of the regiment's companies was enlarged to about 300-strong and a third battalion (initially with just two companies) was created. The Prussian field artillery was restructured on two regiments with three battalions each in 1762. Each battalion consisted of five companies, into which the bombardiers – who no longer had their separate company – were integrated. In 1763, the structure was changed again, with three field artillery regiments, each of two battalions. The size of each company was reduced to 194 rankers and six officers/NCOs. A 4th Field Artillery Regiment, with a large internal establishment comprising ten companies, was formed in 1772. The garrison artillery was also expanded during Frederick's long reign, with three new garrison companies created (at Neisse, Glatz and Schweidnitz) between 1748 and 1750. New units of this kind were raised during the following years in order to man the artillery of important fortifications: Cosel (1756), Colberg (1770), Glogau (1770), Konigsberg (1777), Silberberg (1782) and Graudenz (1784). As a result of this, by the end of Frederick's reign, fourteen companies of garrison artillery were in existence. These had unequal strength, since they were expanded according to circumstances and were composed of men who were deemed unfit for field service.

Frederick the Great is credited with the creation of the first mobile horse artillery, which was not intended primarily to support cavalry but to move rapidly across the battlefield to provide fire support where necessary. Frederick's horse artillery, however, never became independent from the field artillery, and always remained quite small. The first detachment of Prussian horse artillery, created in April 1759, consisted of just three NCOs and forty-two gunners who manned six light 6-pdr guns. A second mounted battery, having this same internal establishment, was created in June 1759. Both horse artillery batteries were destroyed during the pitched battles of 1759, and had to be re-raised from scratch during 1760; they were disbanded definitively soon

Colour plate showing the uniforms of the Prussian Army's quartermasters. From left to right: quartermaster of the infantry, quartermaster of the cuirassiers, quartermaster of the dragoons and quartermaster of the hussars.

after the end of the Seven Years' War. In 1768, Frederick decided to reorganize his horse artillery as a single corps of twenty 6-pdr guns and four howitzers, which was expanded in 1773 to comprise two brigades with ten 6-pdr guns and one 7-pdr howitzer each. Shortly before the outbreak of the War of the Bavarian Succession, the Prussian horse artillery was enlarged to six batteries, each having eight 6-pdr guns and one 7-pdr howitzer.

Frederick the Great always recognized the value of strong fortifications as barriers against the manoeuvres of enemy armies and as places where military matériel could be stockpiled. However, due to his strategies based upon high mobility, the Prussian monarch always placed emphasis upon the construction of temporary field fortifications and detached fortifications placed around fortified garrisons. The Engineer Corps that Frederick inherited from his father was extremely small, consisting of just forty-three specialist officers and a small number of assistants. These were quite proficient, since they had been reorganized by a Dutch engineer officer in Prussian service. During the Seven Years' War, the Engineer Corps consisted of five chief engineers, twenty-one captains, twenty lieutenants and thirteen assistants. These were distributed among the fortresses of Brandenburg-Prussia and were slightly expanded during the following decades, mustering forty-seven officers and thirteen assistants by 1786. The major weakness of the Prussian Engineer Corps was that it did not have a labour force under its command that could build or repair field fortifications. To solve this problem, Frederick the Great decided to raise a regiment of pioneers (combat engineers) in 1742 that was known as the Pionier-Regiment, which consisted of ten sapper companies and two miner companies. In November 1758, due to the general lack of manpower faced by the Prussian Army, Frederick was forced to disband the Pioneer Regiment and to convert its ten sapper companies into the new 49th Fusilier Regiment of the Prussian infantry. The two miner companies were retained in service, with a third company created in 1761 and a fourth one formed in 1783. The miner companies, despite being recruited from civilian miners, never had a high level of proficiency. According to Frederick's tactical views, pioneers were of great use when attacking an entrenched position; they were to follow the infantrymen with shovels, pickaxes and fascines in order to fill up the enemy ditch. The Prussian Army also comprised a small pontoon corps, numbering around fifty men, which was based in Berlin and was originally part of the artillery. It was attached to the miners of the Pioneer Regiment in 1742 before reverting to the artillery in 1774 (it normally accompanied the heavy artillery train).

Uniforms and Equipment

The Prussian artillery wore a uniform based on that of the infantry, including a Prussian blue coat without collar and frontal lapels. This had red turnbacks, Prussian blue cuffs of the 'Prussian' pattern with red-piped flaps and brass buttons. The artillery headgear was a black tricorn with white lace edging and multicolour pompom (yellow/black/red/white from top to bottom). The corner rosettes of the tricorn were multicoloured like the pompom. The artillery uniform was completed by a straw yellow waistcoat and breeches. NCOs had gold lace edging on the tricorn, cuffs and cuff flaps. The officers had unlaced coats, but their tricorns had gold lace edging and their waistcoats were laced in gold. Drummers had coats laced like those of the infantry musicians, with tasselled breast loops and tasselled loops on the sleeves. Their peculiar lace was white with a broad yellow centre and narrow red stripes near each edge. Until 1756, bombardiers wore a low-fronted fusilier-style mitre cap in black leather with voided brass front plate bearing crossed cannon barrels over kettledrums. The mitre also had brass side badges consisting of three-flamed grenades, brass vertical side bands and a flaming grenade finial. The mitre cap was worn by the companies of garrison artillery until the end of Frederick the Great's reign. The garrison artillery had black stocks around the neck, whereas the field artillery had red ones. The small number of horse artillery wore the same uniform as the field artillery, but with leather breeches and gauntlets in addition to long cavalry boots. After 1762, the tricorn hat of the horse artillerymen was given a white cavalry plume (white with black tip for NCOs and white with black base for officers). The shabraque of the horse artillerymen was like that of the dragoons, in Prussian blue with white lace edging and crowned royal cypher in the rounded rear corners. Artillery equipment included a broad-bladed straight short sword, with double-barred brass hilt, carried on a white leather waist-belt. A broad white leather belt was carried over the left shoulder, which supported a wooden and black leather powder flask used for priming; this had brass fittings and a circular badge bearing an embossed crowned royal cypher. Fitted into the leather loops placed on the front of the flask's belt, each artilleryman carried two long vent-prickers – used for piercing a cartridge through the touch hole of a cannon – attached by brass chains to a boss higher on the belt. Muskets were not normally carried by Prussian artillerymen, except for sentry duty. The officers of the Engineer Corps wore a tricorn hat with black cockade, silver loop and silver scalloped edging. Their Prussian blue coats had red folded collar and frontal lapels, red Swedish-pattern cuffs, silver brandenbourgs (loops) on the button-holes with simulated tassel ends (three on each frontal lapel, two below each lapel, two on each cuff and two on each pocket). The outfit was completed by a red waistcoat and breeches. The officers of the Pioneer Regiment wore a tricorn hat with black cockade, silver loop and silver

Officer of the Invalid Corps, a small auxiliary unit made up of soldiers who were no longer fit for active service.

Private of the Invalid Corps.

scalloped edging. Their Prussian blue coats had no collar and frontal lapels, Prussian blue Swedish-pattern cuffs and silver brandenbourgs on the button-holes with tassel ends (six on each frontal lapel, two below each lapel, two on each cuff and two on each pocket). They also wore an orange waistcoat and breeches. The rankers of the Pioneer Regiment had a low-fronted fusilier-style mitre cap in black leather with voided white metal front plate. The plate bore a crowned eagle upon a trophy of arms. The mitre also had white metal side badges consisting of flaming grenades and a white metal four-flamed grenade on the rear. The vertical lace and tuft of the headgear were white. The cloth placed on the back of the mitre was orange. The Prussian blue coat of rankers, differently from that of officers, did not have brandenbourgs; its turnbacks were red. NCOs had a quartered black and white tuft on the headgear, black and white sword knot and silver edging on the cuffs. The pontoneers were dressed like the pioneers until 1773, when they were assigned the same uniform as the field artillery.

Chapter 9

The Freikorps

In addition to the permanent jagers and hussars of the regular army, the Prussian Army of Frederick the Great also included a sizeable number of light corps that were made up of foreign mercenaries: the famous Freikorps, or Free Corps. These were mostly recruited from ex-prisoners of war or from foreign deserters, so in most cases their general quality and discipline were not particularly high. Raised during the Seven Years' War, the Freikorps mostly acted as raiding forces of skirmishers, usually being organized into legions comprising infantry and cavalry as well as jagers and some light guns. Due to their peculiar organizational nature, they could operate as fast-moving and self-contained miniature armies. The Freikorps were frequently employed to conduct special operations, but Frederick did not have a very high opinion of them due to their members being prone to indiscipline and desertion. The Freikorps can be seen as the Prussian response to the Balkan light troops in Habsburg service. While some of their units were commanded by competent officers and thus performed quite well, others were extremely short-lived or conducted themselves poorly in combat. The Freikorps became infamous for their predatory incidents and mutinies, their members usually having decided to fight for Prussia only to have an opportunity for plundering. Consequently, when the Seven Years' War came to an end, they were disarmed at gunpoint and their officers – mere adventurers in most cases – were discharged. Frederick raised twelve new Freikorps for the War of the Bavarian Succession, but these were extremely short-lived and never saw any action. The Freikorps were generally referred to by the name of their commander. Their uniforms and equipment were like those of the regular units, but much simpler and plainer. Some details on each unit of the Freikorps' organizational history and dress follow below.

Freikorps La Noble: Raised in 1756, it consisted of one infantry battalion with a small jager detachment. A second battalion was added in 1760. The uniform of the infantry was as follows: black tricorn with light blue pompom, dark blue coat with light blue frontal lapels and facings, light blue waistcoat and breeches. The jagers had a black leather cap shaped like a fusilier mitre with the royal cypher in white on the front, dark green coat with light green frontal lapels and facings, white brandenbourgs on the button-holes, light green waistcoat and breeches.

The uniforms of Freikorps La Noble; the central figure is a jager, the others are infantrymen.

Freikorps Mayr: Formed in 1756, it consisted of one infantry battalion plus small detachments of jagers and hussars. In 1761, a second battalion was added. The uniform of the infantry comprised the following: black tricorn, dark blue coat without lapels with light blue facings, light blue waistcoat and breeches. The hussars had a black mirliton cap with the royal cypher in white on the front, light blue dolman with white frogging and piping to facings, dark blue pelisse edged with black fur and light blue leggings. The dress of the jagers was like that of the infantry, but in dark green.

The uniforms of Freikorps Mayr; the figure on the left is a jager, the figure on the right a hussar.

Freikorps Kalben: Raised in 1756, it consisted of a single infantry battalion. The corps was expanded with a second infantry battalion in 1759 and a small hussar detachment in 1761. The infantry uniform consisted of black tricorn, dark blue coat without lapels and with light blue facings, light blue waistcoat and breeches. The hussars wore a black mirliton, yellow dolman with red frogging and piping to facings, black pelisse edged with white fur and yellow leggings.

Freikorps Angelelli: Formed in 1756, it comprised a single infantry battalion. The uniform was a black tricorn with light blue pompom, dark blue coat without lapels and with light blue facings, light blue waistcoat and breeches.

Freikorps Chossignon: A single infantry battalion was raised in 1757 and disbanded in 1759. Its dress was as follows: black tricorn, dark blue coat with light blue frontal lapels and cuffs, light blue waistcoat and breeches.

Freikorps Rapin: Raised during 1758 in Magdeburg, mostly from French prisoners of war, it initially consisted of a single infantry battalion. This was supplemented by a second battalion in 1761. The dress consisted of a black tricorn with light blue pompom, dark blue coat without lapels and with light blue facings, light blue waistcoat and breeches.

Freikorps Wunsch: Established in 1758, it initially consisted of a single infantry battalion that was later supplemented by a second. A jager detachment was also created within the unit in 1760. The uniform comprised a black tricorn with light blue pompom, dark blue coat without frontal lapels and with light blue facings, light blue waistcoat and breeches. Light blue lapels were later added to the coat. Jagers wore a black tricorn, dark green coat with red frontal lapels and facings, dark green waistcoat and breeches.

Freikorps du Verger: Organized in 1758 from French deserters, it originally consisted of a single infantry battalion. This was followed by a second battalion in 1760 and a third in 1761. The unit also had a small jager detachment. The uniform of the infantry consisted of the following elements: black tricorn with light blue pompom, dark blue coat with light blue frontal lapels and facings, yellow brandenbourgs on the button-holes, light blue waistcoat and breeches. The jagers had a black tricorn, dark green coat with light green frontal lapels and facings, yellow brandenbourgs on the button-holes, light green *aiguillette* on the right shoulder, light green waistcoat and breeches.

Freikorps Hordt: Raised in 1758, it consisted of two infantry battalions. They were dressed in a black tricorn with a dark blue and light blue pompom, dark blue coat with light blue frontal lapels and facings, white tasselled brandenbourgs on the button-holes, light blue waistcoat and breeches.

Frei-Hussar von Lubomirski: This unit was formed by recruiting Austrian prisoners of war and Prussian deserters. It consisted of three hussar squadrons, but since they never reached their planned establishments the unit was disbanded in late 1758 just a few weeks after its creation. The uniform of the unit was a brown busby with light green bag of cloth, light green dolman with dark green frogging and piping to facings, red pelisse with white fur edging and light green leggings.

Volontaires de Prusse: In December 1758, the Duke of Holstein-Gottorp authorized a major from Hessen-Kassel to raise a Freikorps for service against Prussia in western Germany, but a few days later the unit was transferred to Prussian service by its commander. The Freikorps completed its organization in January 1759 and was funded with financial contributions provided by the Duchy of Berg. The Volontaires de Prusse originally consisted of three musketeer companies (with 126 men each), one jager company and a small detachment of dragoons (forty-eight men). A fourth company of musketeers was raised in May 1759 and substituted the jager company, which was transferred to another Freikorps. The musketeers wore a black tricorn with white edging and half-red and half-white pompom, and a dark blue coat with red folded collar and Swedish-pattern cuffs, red frontal lapels and turnbacks. The jagers had a black tricorn with medium green pompom, medium green coat without frontal lapels but having red folded collar and Swedish-pattern cuffs with red turnbacks. The dragoons wore a black tricorn with dark green cockade and a dark green coat without lapels but having a red folded collar and Swedish-pattern cuffs, with red turnbacks and yellow *aiguillette* on the right shoulder. In February 1760, the Volontaires de Prusse were reorganized on one company of grenadiers, four companies of musketeers, two squadrons of hussars and one detachment of artillery (equipped with two 3-pdrs). The corps also received new uniforms. That of the musketeers was as follows: black tricorn with white edging and light blue pompom, and dark blue coat with red folded collar and frontal lapels, red Swedish-pattern cuffs and turnbacks. The grenadiers were uniformed like the musketeers, but the pompom of their tricorn was red. The hussars were dressed like those of the regular Prussian Army, with black mirliton edged in white, medium blue dolman with white frogging and black facings, medium blue pelisse with black fur edging and medium blue leggings. The Volontaires de Prusse were disbanded in 1763 when the Seven Years' War came to an end, like most of the Freikorps.

Freikorps von Kleist: This was one of the largest and best Freikorps serving under Frederick the Great. It was raised in July 1759 by Friedrich Wilhelm Gottfried Arnd von Kleist, a great friend of the Prussian king. Initially, the unit consisted of just one squadron of volunteer hussars attached to the 1st Hussar Regiment of the Prussian Army, but by 1761 it had become the largest Freikorps in Prussian service (comprising sub-units of infantry, jagers, dragoons and hussars). The original squadron of volunteer hussars comprised just eighty men, mostly Hungarian deserters of the Habsburg Army who were recruited in Dresden. Over time, new squadrons of hussars were recruited, bringing the total to ten, meaning the hussars of Freikorps von Kleist started to have the same numerical consistency of a regular hussar regiment. The ten squadrons, by April 1762, comprised the following elements: forty-one officers, ninety NCOs, ten trumpeters, ten smiths, ten surgeons and 1,000 troopers. Their uniform was quite elegant: brown busby with medium green plume and red bag of cloth, red dolman with white frogging and dark green facings, dark green pelisse with black fur edging and red leggings. The dragoons of Freikorps von Kleist were raised as four squadrons in February 1760, mostly from Prussian volunteers or from foreign deserters. Each squadron consisted of four officers, ten NCOs, one surgeon, one smith, three drummers and 130 troopers. Another six squadrons of dragoons were added to the Freikorps von Kleist during 1760 and 1761. The uniform of the dragoons had a distinctive horse grenadier style: black bearskin medium green skull cap with white metal frontal plate bearing a black Prussian eagle, medium green coat without frontal lapels and folded collar, medium green Swedish-pattern cuffs, white brandenbourgs on the button-holes, medium green turnbacks and white *aiguillette* on the right shoulder. In 1760, a single squadron of Polish uhlans (lancers) was formed within the Freikorps von Kleist. By 1762, following the success of the early lancers, there were ten squadrons of uhlans in Freikorps von Kleist. These wore a uniform that was very similar to that of the regular army's Bosniaken: red fez trimmed with black fur around its base and white plume on the left side, knee-length medium green kaftan decorated on each sleeve with a red horizontal stripe within a wide white band, red edging to the collar and front of the kaftan, two white brandenbourgs on each side of the kaftan's breast, red round cuffs and medium green baggy trousers. The pennon of the lance was medium green and red, with the royal cypher of Frederick the Great embroidered in black. In May 1761, a light infantry battalion, mostly recruited from Croatian deserters of the Austrian army, was created inside Freikorps von Kleist. Known as the Green Croats from the colour of their

The uniforms of Freikorps von Kleist; the figure on the left is a dragoon, the figure on the right a light infantryman of the famous Green Croats.

dress, these performed quite well, so the original battalion (with three companies) was supplemented by a second battalion in 1762. The light infantrymen were dressed in Croatian style and used two different kinds of headgear: a black tricorn with white edging and black cockade or a black mirliton cap with decorative red tassel. Their

Hussar of Freikorps von Kleist.

coat was dark green, without frontal lapels and with red turnbacks, and had white piping to the folded collar and white tasselled brandenbourgs on the button-holes. The dark green waistcoat worn under the coat had white frontal frogging in hussar-style and was used together with a red waist-sash. Trousers were dark green, with white Hungarian knots embroidered on the front. In addition to the Green Croats, the light infantry of Freikorps von Kleist also included a small jager corps. This initially consisted of just a small detachment, which was later expanded to comprise three companies with 100 men each. The jagers' uniform comprised a black tricorn with black cockade, dark green coat with red folded collar and frontal lapels, red Swedishpattern cuffs and turnbacks, dark green waistcoat and breeches. The artillery of Freikorps von Kleist was slowly expanded to comprise one lieutenant, one artificer, one wagon driver, one leather strapmaker, one wheelwright, one wagon maker, one smith, two NCOs, sixteen gunners, six drivers and six bombardiers. These men were equipped with two 6-pdr guns, two 3-pdr guns and one 7-pdr howitzer. Their uniform was quite similar to that of the jagers: a black tricorn with black cockade, dark green coat without frontal lapels and collar, with dark green Prussian-pattern cuffs and light green turnbacks, a dark green waistcoat and breeches.

Légion Britannique: In December 1759, in order to support the war efforts of its ally Frederick the Great, Great Britain decided to fund the raising of some Freikorps on the territory of Hanover. The latter German state was at the time in personal union with Britain, and the British were determined to defend it from French attacks by collaborating with the Prussians. The Hanoverian Army was ordered to provide the cadres for the new Freikorps that later became known as the Légion Britannique. These consisted of forty officers and eighty NCOs who, with their wealth of experience, could effectively train the new corps. By the beginning of April 1760, five battalions of infantry and five squadrons of dragoons had been formed. Each foot battalion consisted of four musketeer companies, while the dragoon squadrons included sizeable numbers of experienced troopers detached from the Hanoverian Army's cavalry regiments. The Légion Britannique was in British pay and served alongside the Hanoverian military forces. Later, each of its infantry battalions was given two 3-pdr guns. The ranks of the Freikorps were mostly recruited from deserters and prisoners of war, as a result of which it suffered from high rates of desertion from the outset. Each of the five battalions and five squadrons that made up the Légion Britannique had a distinctive uniform. The 1st Infantry Battalion had a black tricorn with green cockade, light blue coat with yellow frontal lapels and turnbacks, no collar and yellow Swedish-pattern cuffs, and a yellow waistcoat. The men of the 2nd Infantry Battalion had a black tricorn with green cockade, dark blue coat without frontal lapels and collar, red Swedish-pattern cuffs and turnbacks, and a white waistcoat. The 3rd Infantry Battalion wore a black tricorn with green cockade, white coat with orange frontal lapels and turnbacks, no collar and orange Swedish-pattern cuffs, and an orange waistcoat. The uniform of the 4th Infantry Battalion comprised a black tricorn with green cockade, red coat with light blue frontal lapels and turnbacks, no collar and light blue Swedish-pattern cuffs, and a buff waistcoat. Finally, the 5th Infantry Battalion was allocated a black tricorn with green cockade, red coat without frontal lapels and collar, black Swedish-pattern cuffs and white turnbacks, and a white waistcoat. Meanwhile, the 1st Dragoon Squadron had a black tricorn with green cockade, light blue coat without frontal lapels and collar, white Swedish-pattern cuffs and turnbacks, and yellow *aiguillette* on the right shoulder, plus a white waistcoat and buff breeches. The 2nd Dragoon Squadron had a uniform consisting of a black tricorn with green cockade, dark blue coat without frontal lapels and collar, red Swedish-pattern cuffs and turnbacks, and white *aiguillette* on the right shoulder, a white waistcoat and buff breeches. The 3rd Dragoon Squadron wore a black tricorn with green cockade, white coat without frontal lapels and collar, orange Swedish-pattern cuffs and turnbacks, and yellow *aiguillette* on the right shoulder, an orange waistcoat and buff breeches. The 4th Dragoon Squadron was dressed in a black tricorn with green cockade, red coat without frontal lapels and collar, light blue Swedish-pattern cuffs and turnbacks, and white *aiguillette* on the right shoulder, a white waistcoat and buff breeches. The uniform of the 5th Dragoon Squadron comprised a black tricorn with green cockade, red coat without frontal lapels and collar, black Swedish-pattern cuffs and turnbacks, and white *aiguillette* on the right shoulder, a white waistcoat and buff breeches.

Frei-Husaren von Bauer: Raised in December 1759, this corps initially consisted of a small hussar detachment consisting of fifty men and performing escort duties. It was later expanded and came to comprise a total of four hussar squadrons, each consisting of the following elements: four officers, eight NCOs, one trumpeter, one surgeon, one smith and 108 troopers. A fifth squadron was added in December 1761. The uniform of the original detachment was as follows: brown busby with white plume and red bag of cloth, red dolman with yellow frogging and green facings, green pelisse with black fur edging and red leggings. With the expansion of the corps, the first two squadrons were given the following uniform: black mirliton, dark blue dolman with white frogging and piping to facings, and white leggings. The other three squadrons had a brown busby with a white plume and white bag of cloth, white dolman with white frogging and yellow facings, dark blue pelisse with white fur edging and dark blue leggings.

Freikorps Jeney: Formed in 1760, this comprised one infantry battalion and a small hussar detachment. The infantry was dressed in a black tricorn with light blue pompom, dark blue coat with light blue frontal lapels and facings, light blue waistcoat and breeches. The uniform of the hussar detachment is unknown.

Freikorps Schack: Organized in 1760, this unit consisted of one infantry battalion and a small jager detachment. The infantry wore a black tricorn with light blue pompom, dark blue coat without frontal lapels with light blue facings, and light blue *aiguillette* on the right shoulder, a light blue waistcoat and breeches. The jagers had a black tricorn with light green cockade, dark green coat without frontal lapels with light green facings, and yellow *aiguillette* on the right shoulder, a light green waistcoat and breeches.

Frei-Dragoner von Glasenapp: This was a single regiment of dragoons raised in December 1760. It consisted of five squadrons and comprised the following elements: twenty-one officers, fifty NCOs, fifteen trumpeters, five smiths and 500 troopers. The uniform of the corps was very similar to that worn by the regular dragoons of the Prussian Army: black tricorn with black cockade and white plume, light blue coat without frontal lapels having yellow folded collar, light blue Swedish-pattern cuffs, light blue turnbacks and white *aiguillette* on the right shoulder, a yellow waistcoat and buff breeches.

Freikorps Schony: This unit was raised in March 1761 by an officer of the Wurttemberg Army. Mostly recruited from Hungarian prisoners of war who were in Breslau, it consisted of four grenadier companies and two squadrons of hussars (later increased to three). Freikorps Schony was disbanded in 1763. Each of the hussar squadrons comprised five officers, eight NCOs, one trumpeter, one surgeon, one smith and 102 troopers. The uniform of the hussars consisted of a black mirliton edged in yellow, light blue dolman with red facings and yellow frogging, dark blue pelisse with black fur edging and light blue breeches. Each of the grenadier companies had four officers, nine NCOs, three drummers, two fifers, one surgeon, two carpenters and 150 privates. The uniform of the grenadiers was as follows: black bearskin with brass frontal plate bearing a black Prussian eagle and red bag of cloth piped in yellow on the back, Hungarian style dark blue coat without frontal lapels, but with light blue folded collar with double yellow piping and light blue pointed cuffs, red turnbacks and all button-holes with yellow brandenbourgs, a light blue waistcoat with yellow brandenbourgs, red waist-sash and by light blue trousers with yellow Hungarian knots embroidered on the front. In 1762, the grenadiers' uniform was modified and became much more conventional: light blue mitre cap with white pompom and brass frontal plate, dark blue coat with light blue frontal lapels and Prussian-pattern cuffs, no collar and red turnbacks, and light blue waistcoat.

The uniforms of Freikorps Schony. From left to right: hussar, grenadier and officer of the grenadiers.

Freikorps von Gschray: Organized in April 1761, this comprised a high percentage of French deserters. Initially, it consisted of one infantry battalion (with three companies of musketeers and one company of grenadiers) and six squadrons of dragoons. The infantry battalion had twenty-four officers, sixty NCOs, eighteen

The uniforms of Freikorps von Gschray; the figure on the left is a dragoon, the figure in the centre is an infantryman and the figure on the right is an officer of the infantry.

musicians and 960 privates, while the dragoons had twenty-four officers, forty-eight NCOs, six trumpeters, six smiths and 540 troopers. The uniform of the dragoons was as follows: black tricorn with black cockade and white plume, dark blue coat without collar having black frontal lapels and Swedish-pattern cuffs, yellow fringed shoulder straps, yellow brandenbourgs on the button-holes and red turnbacks. The infantrymen were dressed in a similar manner, the only discernible difference being no cockade on the black tricorn.

Freikorps Heer: Raised in 1761, Freikorps Heer had a very small establishment with just one grenadier company and two musketeer companies (mostly made up of Swiss deserters from the French Army). The uniform comprised a black tricorn with light blue pompom, dark blue coat with light blue frontal lapels and facings, and white tasselled brandenbourgs on the button-holes, a light blue waistcoat and breeches. The grenadier company's headgear was a brown fur cap in Austrian style with red bag of cloth on the back and white metal plate on the front bearing a black Prussian eagle.

Freikorps Bequignoll: This was a single infantry battalion recruited in 1761 from deserters of the French Army. It was dressed with a black tricorn with light blue and white pompom, dark blue coat with light blue frontal lapels and facings, light blue waistcoat and breeches.

Freikorps La Badie: Another single infantry battalion raised in 1761 from deserters of the French Army, its members were dressed as follows: black tricorn with light blue and white pompom, dark blue coat without frontal lapels with light blue facings and white brandenbourgs on the button-holes, a light blue waistcoat and breeches.

Schwarze Legion: This corps, raised in December 1761, consisted of one infantry battalion plus two cavalry squadrons (one of dragoons and one of hussars). The infantry battalion comprised three companies of grenadiers and a small detachment of jagers. The grenadiers were dressed as follows: black mitre cap with brass frontal plate and red tufted pompom, black coat with red frontal lapels and Swedish-pattern cuffs, no collar, yellow *aiguillette* on the right shoulder, yellow brandenbourgs on the button-holes and red turnbacks, and a yellow waistcoat. The jagers wore a black tricorn, black coat with light green frontal lapels and Swedish-pattern cuffs, no collar, yellow *aiguillette* on the right shoulder, yellow brandenbourgs on the button-holes and light green turnbacks, and a light green waistcoat. The dragoons were dressed similarly to the grenadiers, except for the headgear being a black tricorn with red pompom, and they also wore breeches. The hussars had a black mirliton cap, yellow dolman with red frogging and piping to facings, black pelisse with white fur edging and black leggings.

Volontaires Auxiliaires: This unit was formed in 1762 from French and German mercenaries. It never had a good reputation, its members being mostly interested in pillaging. The corps consisted of three grenadier companies, one squadron of uhlans, one squadron of hussars and one squadron of mounted grenadiers. The uhlans were dressed similarly to the Bosniaken: red fez with a white turban wrapped around its base, knee-length grey kaftan with short sleeves, white edging to the collar and front of the kaftan and six white brandenbourgs on each side of the kaftan's breast, and light blue baggy trousers. The pennon of the lance was light blue and yellow. The hussars wore a black busby, dark blue dolman with yellow frogging and facings, dark

The uniforms of the Schwarze Legion. From left to right: officer of the grenadiers, grenadier, jager, hussar and dragoon.

blue pelisse with black fur edging and dark blue breeches. The mounted grenadiers had a black leather helmet in French style, light blue coat with green frontal lapels, green facings and turnbacks, green waistcoat and buff breeches. The foot grenadiers had the same dress as the mounted grenadiers, but wore it with black leather boots.

Frei-Husaren von Barowski: This very short-lived unit, consisting of just one hussar squadron, was disbanded after only a few weeks of service. It wore the following dress: black busby with light green bag of cloth, light green dolman with white frogging and piping to facings, black pelisse with black fur edging and light green leggings.

Bosniak von Petrowski: Another very short-lived corps, disbanded soon after its formation since it never reached its planned establishment of a single uhlan squadron. It was dressed in a red fez having a white turban wrapped around its base, knee-length brown kaftan with short sleeves, green edging to the collar and front of the kaftan and two green brandenbourgs on each side of the kaftan's breast, and brown baggy trousers.

Husaren de Collignon: This unit was raised in 1759 as a small detachment of hussars, tasked with escorting the Prussian governor of Magdeburg. Until its disbandment in 1763, it always consisted of just one lieutenant, one sergeant, two corporals and thirty troopers. The uniform of this corps was quite elegant and similar to that worn by the regular hussars: black busby with white plume and yellow bag of cloth, light blue dolman with white frogging and yellow facings, yellow pelisse edged with black fur and light blue leggings.

Kurmark Landhusaren von Wangenheim: This consisted of a single squadron of volunteer hussars raised in Berlin and comprised the following elements: one commanding officer, two lieutenants, two cornets, ten NCOs, one trumpeter and 100 troopers. Since the squadron was formed from the depots of three regular regiments of hussars (the 2nd, 5th and 6th), its members were initially dressed with the uniforms of their original units. They were given the following dress in 1761: black mirliton with white plume, red dolman with white frogging and piping to facings, red pelisse edged with white fur and red leggings.

Neumark Kammer Hussars: Raised from peasant volunteers in Neumark, this hussar squadron comprised three officers, seven NCOs, one trumpeter and 100 troopers. The unit was disbanded during early 1762. The uniform consisted of a black mirliton cap, dark blue dolman with white frogging and piping to facings, dark blue pelisse edged with white fur and dark blue leggings.

Pommern Landhusaren-Korps: This hussar squadron was raised from peasant volunteers in Pomerania, with four officers, eight NCOs, one trumpeter, one blacksmith, one surgeon and 100 troopers. A second squadron was added in October 1758. The uniform of the 1st Squadron was as follows: black mirliton with white plume, light blue

Troopers of the Kurmark Landhusaren von Wangenheim (left) and Husaren de Collignon (right).

dolman with white frogging and red facings, dark blue pelisse with white fur edging and light blue leggings. The men of the 2nd Squadron wore a black mirliton, dark blue dolman with white frogging and red facings, dark blue pelisse with black fur edging and dark blue breeches. In April 1762, the Kurmark Landhusaren von Wangenheim, Neumark Kammer Hussars and Pommern Landhusaren-Korps were amalgamated to form a single unit known as the Provinzial-Husaren-Bataillon von Hohendorff, which consisted of four squadrons, each of which wore its original uniform.

Chapter 10

The Allied Contingents

During the Seven Years' War, several German states of the Holy Roman Empire were allies of Prussia and thus supported Frederick the Great's military endeavours. Leasing military units to foreign powers such as Prussia, Great Britain or the Netherlands was an important source of income for several German princedoms during the eighteenth century: the Landgraviate of Hesse-Kassel, for example, rented out part of its professional armed forces several times because it allowed the rulers of the state to maintain a large standing army over several decades (which was difficult to achieve from a financial point of view). The leasing of professional fighting units took place according to the Subsidy System, which was introduced by William of Orange in 1672 for the Dutch army. This was based on rental contracts signed between the Netherlands and other states, according to which the Dutch paid a rental fee to the German princedoms, the wages of the troops that had been hired and provided them with all their supplies. In exchange for this, the German princedoms had to keep the hired units up to strength by sending a sufficient number of new recruits, but were freed (albeit temporarily) from the high costs of maintaining a standing army. After the outbreak of the Seven Years' War, Britain decided to assemble an army in western Germany to support Frederick the Great in his struggle against France and Austria. This force, known as His Britannic Majesty's Army in Germany, was paid by the British and was mostly tasked with protecting Hanover. This army consisted of contingents from various states: a British expeditionary force, the Hanoverian Army (supported by a small subsidiary contingent from the neighbouring state of Buckenburg, paid by Hanover), the army of Hesse-Kassel and the army of Brunswick. The latter German princedoms had been allies of Britain for many years and had provided troops to the British government under the Subsidy System during the War of the Austrian Succession. After the Seven Years' War, they continued to be allies of the British and provided significant military contingents to them during the American Revolution of 1775–83. Listed below are details of the organization and uniforms of the units from each of the German states that supported Prussia during the Seven Years' War and contributed to the formation of His Britannic Majesty's Army in Germany.

Hanoverian grenadier of the Fussgarde Regiment.

Hanoverian trooper of the Grenadieren zu Pferde Regiment.

Hanover

The Hanoverian Army, despite wearing red uniforms that were quite similar to those of the British Army, had very little in common with the latter. Among the military forces of the German princedoms, Hanover's was one of the largest and most experienced, having fought against the French on several occasions. In

The uniforms of the Hanoverian Jager Corps. From left to right: mounted jager, foot jager and grenadier.

1756, the infantry of the Hanoverian Army consisted of twenty-seven battalion-sized regiments: twenty-four of musketeers and three of grenadiers. Each regiment consisted of seven companies, with 122 officers and men each, while each musketeer company – albeit only administratively – included eight grenadiers who were detached to provide the personnel for the formation of a composite grenadier company. The various composite grenadier companies were assembled into the three regiments of grenadiers, which had elite status. The infantry of the Hanoverian Army also included one guard regiment, known as the Fussgarde. This had a large establishment with two battalions, and its grenadiers were not detached from their parent companies (since they were tasked with bodyguard duties). Each Hanoverian infantry regiment had a staff of nineteen officers and NCOs, except for the Fussgarde, which had a staff of twenty. In 1758, another two musketeer regiments, with only five companies each and without grenadiers, were added to the existing units. The

Carabinier of Scheither Freikorps (left) and trooper of Luckner's Hussars (right). Both units were in Hanoverian service.

Hanoverian musketeers had red uniforms that resembled, in their cut, those of the Prussian infantry: black tricorn with white edging, black cockade and pompom in regimental colour, a red coat without collar and with frontal lapels in regimental colour, Prussian-pattern cuffs and turnbacks, brass buttons and white brandenbourgs on the button-holes, a waistcoat in regimental colour, straw-coloured breeches, white

The uniforms of Hesse-Kassel's 1st Garde Regiment. From left to right: officer, NCO, drummer, grenadier and musketeer. The fur cap replaced the mitre cap as the headgear of grenadiers after the Seven Years' War.

Hesse-Kassel grenadier of the Graf von Hessenstein Infantry Regiment.

Hesse-Kassel officer of the Leib Infantry Regiment. (*Anne S.K. Brown Collection*)

Hesse-Kassel NCO of the Leib Infantry Regiment. (*Anne S.K. Brown Collection*)

stockings and buff leather equipment. Grenadiers were uniformed like musketeers, but their headgear was a mitre cap entirely made of cloth, with facing-coloured front bearing embroidered decorations and a red bag of cloth on the back. The point of the mitre was surmounted by a pompom in regimental colour. The elite Fussgarde had dark blue as its regimental colour, golden brandenbourgs (also on the button-holes of the waistcoat) and golden piping to facings.

The cavalry of the Hanoverian Army comprised eight cuirassier regiments and four dragoon regiments. The cuirassier units had six companies each, which were assembled into two squadrons, each squadron mustering 361 officers and men. One of the cuirassier regiments had guard status and was known as the Leib-Regiment, or Bodyguard Regiment. The dragoon units were considerably larger than those of cuirassiers, with each of them having eight companies assembled into four squadrons. One of the dragoon regiments had guard status and was known as the Grenadieren zu Pferde, or Horse Grenadiers, despite being a dragoon corps. The two guard regiments of the Hanoverian cavalry had distinctive red uniforms. The men of the Leib-Regiment wore a black tricorn with silver edging and black cockade, red coat without collar and with frontal lapels in dark blue, red Swedish-pattern cuffs, dark blue turnbacks and silver buttons, a straw-coloured waistcoat and breeches. The Grenadieren zu Pferde had a mitre cap entirely made of cloth, with black front bearing embroidered decorations and red bag of cloth on the back. The point of the mitre was surmounted by a red pompom. The uniform also included a red coat without collar and with frontal lapels in black, black Swedish-pattern cuffs, red turnbacks, golden buttons and golden *aiguillette* on the right shoulder, a straw-coloured waistcoat and breeches. The Hanoverian cuirassiers, despite their denomination, were not equipped with cuirasses, so they were dressed more or less like the dragoons. Their uniform consisted of the following elements: black tricorn edged in white with black cockade, white coat without frontal lapels and collar, with Swedish-pattern cuffs and turnbacks in regimental colour, white metal buttons, straw-coloured waistcoat and breeches. Dragoons had frontal lapels on their coats, in regimental colour. One company in each dragoon regiment, being designated as mounted grenadiers, had a mitre cap in white.

Like the Prussian Army, the Hanoverian Army included light infantry and light cavalry units belonging to two main categories: the regular light corps and the Freikorps. At the beginning of the Seven Years' War, the regular Hanoverian troops did not include any light unit. Then in May 1757, a Jager Corps consisting of just two companies was raised. One company was of foot jagers and the other of mounted jagers. The Hanoverian jagers were expanded with the addition of two foot companies in 1758, followed by another mounted company in 1759. The regular light

Hesse-Kassel grenadier of the Leib Infantry Regiment. (*Anne S.K. Brown Collection*)

Hesse-Kassel musketeer of the Leib Infantry Regiment. (*Anne S.K. Brown Collection*)

Hesse-Kassel pioneer of the Leib Infantry Regiment. (*Anne S.K. Brown Collection*)

Hesse-Kassel standard-bearer of the Leib Infantry Regiment. (*Anne S.K. Brown Collection*)

infantrymen distinguished themselves on several occasions, especially after the Jager Corps was put under the orders of Colonel Freytag, and was consequently expanded to comprise six foot companies and six mounted companies. In 1762, the Jager Corps was consolidated as a single battalion with four companies, after having absorbed a Freikorps – known as Stockhausen's Jagers – consisting of one grenadier company and four jager companies (two on foot and two mounted). The first Freikorps to enter Hanoverian service was a small detachment of hussars – known as Luckner's Hussars – that had previously been in Dutch service. Expanded to two companies in 1758, the hussars had the opportunity to show their skill as skirmishers and explorers, and by 1760 they consisted of eight companies assembled into four squadrons. In May 1758, a new Freikorps was raised for Hanoverian service by Captain Scheither. This initially comprised a single company, but by 1761 it had been expanded to include the following: two companies of grenadiers, one company of jagers, four companies of carabiniers (heavy cavalry) and one detachment of artillery. Members of the regular Jager Corps were dressed as follows: black tricorn, dark green coat with dark green frontal facings, Swedish-pattern cuffs and white metal buttons, dark green waistcoat and straw-coloured breeches. Foot jagers had black gaiters, while mounted jagers had black leather boots. The grenadiers of Stockhausen's Jagers wore a peculiar dark green mitre cap similar in shape and dimensions to that used by the Prussian fusiliers. Luckner's Hussars were originally dressed in a black mirliton, dark green dolman with yellow frogging and piping to facings, dark green pelisse with black fur edging and red leggings with yellow Hungarian knots embroidered on the front. This dress, however, was later discontinued because it was too similar to that worn by a French light cavalry unit. The following new uniform was introduced: black busby with red bag of cloth, white dolman with yellow frogging and piping to facings, red pelisse with black fur edging and white leggings with yellow Hungarian knots embroidered on the front. The carabiniers of Freikorps Scheither wore a black tricorn with green cockade, white Kollet coat in Prussian style with green edging to the front and turnbacks and green Swedish-pattern cuffs, a green waistcoat with white edging to the front and straw-coloured breeches. Both the grenadiers and jagers of the corps wore green coats without frontal lapels and with green turnbacks, while the folded collar and Swedish-pattern cuffs were also green (with double zig-zag piping in white for grenadiers). The uniform was completed by a straw-coloured waistcoat and breeches. The grenadiers wore a brown fur cap, while the jagers had a standard black tricorn. Each company of grenadiers and jagers included a detachment of six sappers, who wore a mitre cap similar to that of the Prussian fusiliers with a green turban wrapped around its main body. The artillery of Freikorps Scheither was dressed like the regular gunners of the Hanoverian Army. At the beginning of the

Hesse-Kassel drummer of the Leib Infantry Regiment. (*Anne S.K. Brown Collection*)

Uniforms of the Hesse-Kassel Fusilier Regiment von Lossberg. (*Anne S.K. Brown Collection*)

Uniforms of the Hesse-Kassel Fusilier Regiment von Dittfurth. (*Anne S.K. Brown Collection*)

Uniforms of the Hesse-Kassel Fusilier Regiment von Lossburg. (*Anne S.K. Brown Collection*)

Uniforms of the Hesse-Kassel Musketeer Regiment von Donop. (*Anne S.K. Brown Collection*)

Uniforms of the Hesse-Kassel Musketeer Regiment Prinz Carl. (*Anne S.K. Brown Collection*)

Uniforms of the Hesse-Kassel Jager Corps. (*Anne S.K. Brown Collection*)

Hesse-Kassel trooper
of the dragoons.

Seven Years' War, the Hanoverian Army's artillery consisted of six companies, each with sixty-seven officers and men, but these were soon reorganized into four field artillery brigades with two or three companies each. The artillerymen wore a black tricorn edged in yellow, iron grey coats without frontal lapels and collar, red Swedish-pattern cuffs and turnbacks, iron grey waistcoat and straw-coloured breeches.

Attached to the Hanoverian Army was a small subsidiary contingent provided by the state of Buckenburg, which comprised one infantry regiment, one jager company, one carabinier company and one artillery company. The infantry wore a black tricorn with white edging and red-over-white pompom, dark blue coat without frontal lapels with red facings and turnbacks, white waistcoat and breeches. The single grenadier company of the infantry regiment had a brass-fronted fusilier mitre cap as its headgear. The jagers wore a black tricorn, dark green coat with yellow folded collar and Swedish-pattern cuffs, no frontal lapels and dark green turnbacks, yellow waistcoat and dark green breeches. The carabiniers had a metal cuirass and helmet painted in black; the latter, curiously, had a band of dark brown fur wrapped around its main body. The outfit was completed by a black coat with red facings and turnbacks, straw-coloured waistcoat and breeches. The artillerymen wore a black tricorn, iron grey coat without frontal lapels but with black cuffs and red turnbacks, white waistcoat and iron grey breeches.

Hesse-Kassel

The Landgraviate of Hesse-Kassel, located in western Germany south of Hanover, had one of the best and largest professional armies of the Holy Roman Empire. In terms of quality and numbers, the troops of Hesse-Kassel were inferior in Germany only to those of the four major states (Austria, Prussia, Bavaria and Saxony). At the beginning of the Seven Years' War, the Hesse-Kassel infantry consisted of twelve battalion-sized regiments (eleven of musketeers and one of grenadiers), each of which had ten companies. In 1760, the ten companies of each musketeer unit were consolidated into eight, assembled into two battalions with four companies each. At the same time, the practice of drawing eight men from each musketeer company to serve as grenadiers ceased and the two remaining companies from each musketeer regiment were consolidated to form six independent grenadier battalions. In 1756, just one of the infantry regiments had guard status, the Leibgarde zu Fuss. In 1760, however, a new guard infantry regiment was raised and the single grenadier regiment was also given guard status. Following these organizational changes, the new guard infantry regiment formed in 1760 became the 1st Garde, the grenadier regiment became the 2nd Garde and the Leibgarde zu Fuss became the 3rd Garde. The 1st

Garde had just one battalion, while the 2nd Garde and 3rd Garde had two battalions each. After these changes, one line infantry regiment was elevated to guard status and became the 4th Garde (also known as the Leib-Regiment). Two of the remaining line infantry regiments were later transformed from musketeer into fusilier units, but this had little practical consequence. As a result of the above, in 1763 the Hesse-Kassel infantry consisted of the following units: four guard regiments, seven musketeer regiments and two fusilier regiments. The uniform of the Hesse-Kassel infantry was quite similar to that worn by the contemporary Prussian foot regiments: black tricorn with white edging and pompom in regimental colour, dark blue coat with frontal lapels and turnbacks in regimental colour, no collar and Prussian-pattern cuffs in regimental colour, a waistcoat and breeches in regimental colour. Most of the units had white brandenbourgs on the button-holes, their number, shape and disposition distinguishing the various regiments. The brandenbourgs of guard regiments were tasselled. Belt equipment was white leather. Grenadiers had Prussian-style mitre caps with pompom in regimental colour and cloth in regimental colour on the back. The embossed frontal plate was white metal. The two fusilier regiments had Prussian-style fusilier caps, without pompom but with brass frontal plate.

The Hesse-Kassel cavalry consisted of horse and dragoon regiments. The four horse regiments, which were heavy cavalry units of cuirassiers but were not equipped with metal cuirasses, had two squadrons each, while the two dragoon regiments had four squadrons each. In 1760, as part of the general reorganization of the Hesse-Kassel military that took place that year, a small Garde du Corps mounted bodyguard was formed and added to the cavalry establishment. This new unit, however, performed only ceremonial duties. Before 1760, the horse regiments wore a black tricorn with black cockade and golden edging, white frock coat with folded collar, Swedish-pattern cuffs in regimental colour and golden piping to facings, white breeches and black leather boots. They were then given a Prussian-style uniform consisting of a black tricorn with black cockade and golden edging, buff-coloured Kollet with facings in regimental colour and golden piping to the facings, buff-coloured breeches and black leather boots. In 1760, the Hesse-Kassel heavy cavalry was issued with metal cuirasses painted black. The dragoon regiments were uniformed like those of the Prussian Army: black tricorn with black cockade and white plume, having the base in regimental colour, dark blue coat with frontal lapels and turnbacks in regimental colour, no collar and Swedish-pattern cuffs in regimental colour, a straw-coloured waistcoat and buff-coloured breeches. In 1760, the colour of the coats was changed from dark blue to light blue. In addition to the cuirassiers and dragoons described above, the Hesse-Kassel cavalry also featured a regiment of hussars. This had a quite peculiar history, since it had been formed in 1744 when Hesse-Kassel

Uniforms of the Hesse-Kassel artillery. (*Anne S.K. Brown Collection*)

leased some of its military units to Great Britain in order to fight in Scotland during the Jacobite Rising. The unit was created as a single squadron with two companies, but in 1756 it was expanded to comprise two squadrons. With the reorganization of 1760, the Husaren-Korps came to comprise four squadrons. The uniform of the Hesse-Kassel hussars was as follows: brown busby with red bag of cloth, light blue dolman with yellow frogging and red facings, light blue pelisse edged with brown fur and light blue leggings.

The Hesse-Kassel regular light troops consisted of a small jager corps with two foot companies, which, in August 1759, were supplemented by two mounted companies. The jagers wore a black tricorn, dark green coat with red frontal lapels and turnbacks, red folded collar and Swedish-pattern cuffs, a dark green waistcoat and breeches. A single Freikorps was raised by Hesse-Kassel during the Seven Years' War, this being a light infantry battalion known as the Chasseur Battalion von Rall. Its members wore a black tricorn with white edging and green pompom, light blue coat with green frontal lapels and turnbacks, no collar and green Swedish-pattern cuffs, a green waistcoat and breeches. The Hesse-Kassel artillery consisted of just two companies in 1756, which were increased to three in 1757 and five in 1760. These

Uniforms of the Brunswick infantry.

were responsible for the heavy pieces only, since the battalion guns of the infantry units were manned by a few gunners attached to the foot regiments. By the end of the Seven Years' War, the battalion guns were manned by four autonomous artillery companies. All the Hesse-Kassel artillerymen were uniformed as follows: black tricorn with white edging and red pompom, dark blue coat with red frontal lapels and turnbacks, red folded collar and Prussian-pattern cuffs, dark blue waistcoat and

Brunswick standard-bearer of Infantry Regiment Specht. (*Anne S.K. Brown Collection*)

breeches. The Hesse-Kassel regular military were supported by a territorial militia known as the Landmiliz, which was mostly tasked with performing garrison and police duties. The militia was originally organized on three infantry regiments, but in 1760 these were transformed into one garrison grenadier battalion and three garrison

Brunswick officer of Infantry Regiment von Rhetz. (*Anne S.K. Brown Collection*)

battalions (all with four companies each). The Hesse-Kassel militiamen wore a black tricorn with white edging, dark blue coat without frontal lapels and collar, with red turnbacks and Swedish-pattern cuffs, a straw-coloured waistcoat and breeches.

Brunswick

The small state of Brunswick, located in the heart of central Germany, was a loyal ally of both Great Britain and Prussia well before the outbreak of the Seven Years' War. It had small but efficient military forces, with significant combat experience. The Brunswick infantry consisted of four battalion-sized regiments, each of which comprised five musketeer companies and one grenadier company. The grenadier companies of each unit, in time of war, were usually detached from their parent regiments and assembled together in order to form two provisional grenadier battalions with two companies each. In 1759, the two grenadier battalions were expanded to three and became permanent corps, independent from the line infantry. During the same year, the Brunswick infantry was also enlarged with the formation of two new battalions: an elite one with guard status (the Leib-Grenadiere Garde) and a fusilier one having garrison duties (the Fusilier-Bataillon von Volschen). The general appearance of the Brunswick infantry was very 'Prussian', its uniform consisting of the following elements: black tricorn with black cockade and white edging, dark blue coat with frontal lapels and turnbacks in regimental colour, folded collar and Swedish-pattern cuffs in regimental colour, white waistcoat and breeches. The grenadier companies and units wore a mitre cap, which had the cloth on the back in regimental colour, a white metal frontal plate and a pompom in regimental colour. Belt equipment was white for all foot units.

The Brunswick cavalry of 1756 consisted of a single unit, a dragoon regiment with four companies. In 1759, this was converted into a carabinier regiment and was expanded to six companies assembled into three squadrons. Until 1759, the uniform of the corps was as follows: black tricorn with black cockade, golden scalloped edging and yellow pompom, red coat without frontal lapels but with yellow folded collar and Swedish-pattern cuffs, yellow turnbacks and brandenbourgs on the button-holes, a yellow waistcoat and breeches. A new dress, very similar to that of the Prussian cuirassiers, was introduced in 1759: black tricorn with black cockade, golden scalloped edging and yellow pompom, a buff-coloured Kollet with red facings, buff-coloured breeches and black leather boots. The uniform was worn with a metal cuirass painted black. In 1759, the Brunswick cavalry was expanded with the formation of a new hussar regiment, having four companies, which was expanded to six in 1761. The unit was raised with British funds but became an important component of the Brunswick

Brunswick standard-bearer of Infantry Regiment von Rhetz. (*Anne S.K. Brown Collection*)

Brunswick standard-bearer of Infantry Regiment Prinz Friedrich. (*Anne S.K. Brown Collection*)

Colour plate showing the uniforms of the Brunswick military forces. From left to right: dragoon, musketeer of Infantry Regiment Specht, light infantryman of Battalion von Barner and foot jager.

armed forces. Its uniform consisted of a tall grey busby with yellow bag of cloth and white plume with red base, yellow dolman with white frontal frogging and edging to facings and a violet collar, violet pelisse with white fur edging and yellow leggings with white Hungarian knots embroidered on the front.

Until 1759, Brunswick's forces did not include any regular light unit, but in that year a small jager corps was formed. This comprised three foot companies and two mounted companies. It was expanded with the addition of one foot company

Brunswick officer of the dragoons.
(*Anne S.K. Brown Collection*)

Brunswick foot jager. (*Anne S.K. Brown Collection*)

Brunswick officer of Battalion von Barner. (*Anne S.K. Brown Collection*)

Brunswick private from the jager company of Battalion von Barner. (*Anne S.K. Brown Collection*)

and one mounted company in 1762. The corps also had two light artillery pieces, manned by thirteen gunners. The Brunswick jagers wore a black tricorn with green pompom, medium green coat without frontal lapels but with red folded collar and turnbacks (straw-coloured for mounted companies), a medium green waistcoat and straw-coloured breeches. In 1762, a new light infantry battalion, known as the Light Infantry Battalion von Barner, was raised. This wore a black tricorn edged in white with white and yellow pompom, dark blue coat without frontal lapels but with black folded collar, Swedish-pattern cuffs and red turnbacks, a white waistcoat and breeches. The first Freikorps in Brunswick service was raised in 1762. Known as the Volontaires Auxiliares de Bronswick, it comprised three companies of grenadiers and three companies of cavalry (one of mounted grenadiers, one of hussars and one of Bosniaken). It was mostly recruited from Balkan deserters or prisoners of war from the Austrian army. The foot grenadiers wore a mitre cap similar to that of the Prussian fusiliers, light blue coat with green facings, green waistcoat and straw-coloured breeches. The mounted grenadiers were dressed like the foot ones, but their coats were dark blue instead of light blue. The hussars had a tall black busby with yellow bag of cloth, dark blue dolman with yellow frontal frogging and facings, dark blue pelisse with black fur edging and dark blue leggings with yellow Hungarian knots embroidered on the front. The Bosniaken were dressed like those of the Prussian Army, including a dark grey kaftan with white trimming and light blue baggy trousers. Their headgear was a red fez with a white turban wrapped around its body. The Brunswick artillery consisted of just three companies during the Seven Years' War, its members being uniformed as follows: black tricorn with yellow edging, dark blue coat without frontal lapels and collar but with red Swedish-pattern cuffs and turnbacks, a straw-coloured waistcoat and breeches.

Select Bibliography

Dorn, Gunther and Engelmann, Joachim, *The Cavalry Regiments of Frederick the Great, 1756–1763* (Schiffer Publishing, 1989).

Dorn, Gunther and Engelmann, Joachim, *The Infantry Regiments of Frederick the Great, 1756–1763* (Schiffer Publishing, 1989).

Duffy, Cristopher, *The Army of Frederick the Great* (The Emperor's Press, 2008).

Friedrich, Wolfgang, *Die Uniformen der Kurfurstlich Sachsischen Armee, 1683–1763* (Sachsischen Militargeschichte, 1998).

Funcken, Fred and Funcken, Liliane, *L'uniforme et les Armes des Soldats des Etats-Unis: La cavallerie et l'artillerie* (Casterman, 1979).

Funcken, Fred and Funcken, Liliane, *L'uniforme et les Armes des Soldats des Etats-Unis: L'infanterie et la marine* (Casterman, 1979).

Grant, Charles Stewart, *From Pike to Shot, 1685 to 1720* (Wargames Research Group, 1986).

Haythornthwaite, Philip, *Frederick the Great's Army (1): Cavalry* (Osprey Publishing, 1991).

Haythornthwaite, Philip, *Frederick the Great's Army (2): Infantry* (Osprey Publishing, 1991).

Haythornthwaite, Philip, *Frederick the Great's Army (3): Specialist Troops* (Osprey Publishing, 1992).

Hofschroer, Peter, *The Hanoverian Army of the Napoleonic Wars* (Osprey Publishing, 1989).

Hohrath, Daniel, *The Uniforms of the Prussian Army under Frederick the Great from 1740 to 1786* (Verlag Militaria, 2011).

Kling, Steven, *The Army of Holstein-Gottorp in the Great Northern War*, in 'Great Northern War Compendium', vol. I (THGC Publishing, 2015).

Kling, Steven, *The Electorate of Hanover and its Army during the Great Northern War*, in 'Great Northern War Compendium', vol. II (THGC Publishing, 2015).

Kuhn, August, *Brandenburg-Prussia's Army under King Frederick I* (Robert Hall, 2001).

Kuhn, August, *The Hanoverian Armies during the War of the Spanish Succession* (Editions Brokaw, 1991).

Kuhn, August, *The Military Forces of the Duchies of Schlesswig-Holstein-Gottorp and the Military States of the Upper Saxon Circle* (Editions Brokaw, 1991).

Mollo, John, *Uniforms of the American Revolution in Colour* (Blandford Press, 1975).

Querengasser, Alexander, *Die Armee Augusts des Starken im Nordischen Krieg* (Zeughaus Verlag, 2013).

Querengasser, Alexander, *The Saxon Army in the Great Northern War*, in 'Great Northern War Compendium', vol. I (THGC Publishing, 2015).

Reid, Stuart, *Frederick the Great's Allies, 1756–1763* (Osprey Publishing, 2010).

Reid, Stuart, *King George's Army, 1740–1793 (1)* (Osprey Publishing, 1995).

Reid, Stuart, *King George's Army, 1740–1793 (2)* (Osprey Publishing, 1995).

Reid, Stuart, *King George's Army, 1740–1793 (3)* (Osprey Publishing, 1996).

Schorr, Dan, *The Saxon Polish Army during the Great Northern War* (Editions Brokaw, 1987).

Schreckengost, Gary, *The Battles of Frederick the Great* (CreateSpace Independent Publishing, 2017).

Showalter, Dennis, *Frederick the Great: a Military History* (Frontline Books, 2020).

Smith, Digby and Riley, Kevin F., *An Illustrated Encyclopedia of Uniforms from 1775–1783: The American Revolutionary War* (Lorenz Books, 2008).

Summerfield, Stephen, *The Prussian Army of the Great Northern War*, in 'Great Northern War Compendium', vol. II (THGC Publishing, 2015).

The Company of Military Historians, *Military Uniforms in America: the Era of the American Revolution* (Presidio Press, 1975).

Index